Memoirs from the Psych Ward

By

Hatake Hugo aka **Ernst-William Hertz**

For My Mother

Thank you, Mom, for being the unwavering foundation of my life. Through every twist and turn, you have stood by my side, offering your love, patience, and strength. You have been my caretaker, my confidant, and my greatest supporter, even when the weight of the world bore down on both of us.

Your sacrifices and endless dedication have shaped the person I am today. You've shown me the true meaning of resilience, compassion, and unconditional love.

This book is as much yours as it is mine. Without your guidance and care, none of this would have been possible. From the depths of my heart, thank you for everything you've done for me—every single day of my life.

With all my love,

William.

Contents

Foreword

The following book is a collection of my personal memoirs, crafted from the best extent of my memories. I have carefully reviewed every page multiple times to ensure the highest quality possible.

Each person named in this memoir has either given their permission for their name to be used or provided a pseudonym for me to use in the book.

While the stories told are genuine, they may be exaggerated, as this is an autofictional book and not a strict autobiography.

I would like to extend my gratitude to everyone who made it possible for me to write this book and to everyone reading it.

Thank you.

Introduction

Hello everyone reading this book—this is Ernst-William Hertz, also known as Hatake Hugo, speaking! I'm going to tell you the story of my life.

When does my story truly begin? Is it at birth or with my earliest memories? Organic memories or what I've been told about my first steps in life? What's the difference? Shouldn't you believe all the memories in your head? Why did this suddenly take a philosophical turn? It's strange how we can be so sure something happened a certain way, only to later realise it's due to someone else placing that thought—or memory—in our heads.

Let's start with a situation that took place in 2022, when I was in maximum security custody in Gothenburg, accused of murder. During this time, I was devising a diabolic plan for what to do with 3 billion Swedish krona (SEK).

One day, my pen broke, and I wasn't allowed a replacement due to threats I had made to the prison wardens, promising to shank them with a sharpened pencil. Desperate, I self-inflicted a wound on my lip with the remaining pencil and began writing the rest of my business plans with my own blood, using a Q-tip like an old-fashioned quill dipped in ink.

Why did I make a business plan on how to use 3 billion SEK? Well, I had nothing to do for months. The only things at my disposal were a pen, paper, and my brainpower, which I used to channel all my accumulated information and knowledge onto paper.

I will release all of the paperwork that I conducted to the public and go further into detail later on in the book. Those topics include but are not limited to:

SCS = Social Credit Score

Turning real-life into an MMORPG* where stats are given for different tasks—done by implementing systems into governments involving 4000p cameras.

Massive multi online role-playing game.

CT = ChinaTown

Establishing a foundation where pieces/bricks are built that are utilised as Lego pieces in order to put together houses and mass-produce them to build towns in rural areas where there isn't housing available.

Will incorporate SCS's surveillance system into CT with 4k cameras in order to utilise the initial CT as a role model and demo-display for other governments to buy and implement SCS in their countries.

LMC = Legal Medicinal Cocaine

Liberating a South American country at a time by lobbying political movements to legalise the production and exportation of medicinal cocaine—assembling politicians in a European country to start medicinal clinics to see if it's suitable as a treatment for depression, allowing users all over Europe to get treatment in said European country (Sweden in my example) and to bring home 30 days worth of medicine to their own country. This would allow Sweden to generate a lot of tourist dollars, and cocaine would be shipped from SA to CN and placed in GPS-chipped usable containers.

Pharmacy and psychiatrists are supposed to be harboured in a CT located in northern Sweden.

BB = BestBuds

My own love and hope—which I once owned 17 domain names* for, a cannabis movement that no longer exists. A to-be international smuggling operation with a legal facade that would be suitable for acting as a front figure for the cannabis movement in Europe.

Producing hash, clothes and blunt cones in India, rolling paper and LSD in China. *Internet website names.

As I reflect on these grand plans and ideas, I can't help but think about how they are rooted in the experiences that shaped me. The journey to where I am now is anything but straightforward. From the moments of clarity in the midst of chaos to the times when my path seemed uncertain, every experience contributed to the person I've become.

My childhood was a blend of contradictions. On one hand, there was an endless curiosity and a love for the fantastical worlds of Magic: The Gathering. On the other, there were the harsh realities of a father who was often absent and a brother who chose a dangerous path by joining the French Foreign Legion. I remember the comfort I found in the structure and strategy of card games, which seemed like a complete contrast to the unpredictability of my life.

During my teenage years, the streets of our neighbourhood were both a playground and a battleground. The allure of quick money through dealing drugs became an undeniable temptation, mirroring my brother's descent into the underworld. It was a time of reckless decisions and fleeting highs, each representing a temporary escape from the void left by my father's absence.

Yet, amidst the turmoil, there was always a spark of creativity and hope. This light shines most brightly through my passion for entrepreneurship. The business plans I drafted, often in the most unconventional of circumstances, were a testament to my belief in a better future. Whether it was envisioning a socially integrated surveillance system or dreaming of revolutionising the medicinal use of cocaine, these ideas were born from a deep-seated desire to make a mark on the world.

The transition from these chaotic years to my time in maximum security custody was overwhelming. In 2022, under the weight of murder accusations, my world narrowed to the confines of a cell in Gothenburg. It was here, in the depths of isolation, that I found an unexpected outlet for my ambitions. With a broken pen and nothing but time, I started drafting detailed business plans using my own blood and a makeshift feather pen. The act was both a rebellion against my circumstances and a testament to my relentless drive.

Why did I choose to focus on how I would utilise 3 billion SEK? The truth is, it was a way to channel my restless mind and give purpose to my days. Stripped of freedom, I still had my intellect and creativity. These plans became a lifeline, a way to stay connected to the world outside and envision a future beyond the bars.

As I release these documents to the public, I hope they serve as more than just a record of my thoughts. They are a window into the mind of someone who, despite being surrounded by darkness, never stopped striving for light. Each idea, whether grandiose or grounded, is a piece of my journey—a journey that I will continue to unravel and explore in the chapters ahead.

Childhood (Birth – Age of 7)

Now let's start from the beginning of my life now that you've gotten a teaser of what lies ahead.

I was supposedly born in Stockholm, something I, of course, don't remember but have no reason to disbelieve. Why would someone lie about such a trivial matter as where you were born? Who? My own family? Why would they trick me about that? There shouldn't be any reason, so let's believe that I was born in Stockholm.

Some people question every statement from their surroundings. I'm not here to say whether that's good or bad—everyone lives their life their own way. I have my way, and you have yours.

I was born on December 5, 1998, in Värmdö, Stockholm, to a family of six—four children and our parents. My siblings, in order of birth, are:

- Axel-Christian Hertz born 1985
- Beatrice Hertz born 1990

- Carl-Axel Hertz 1995

- Calle Hertz (born 1996 as Carl-Philip Hertz)

Our parents were Pia Janzon, who changed her surname to Hertz before I was born, and Peter Hertz. We lived in Stockholm until I was 1½ years old, then moved to Löderup, near Ystad. My memories begin in Löderup since I was too young to remember Stockholm. However, there is a picture of me in my early acting days, playing baby Jesus fresh out of baptism at Fisksätra Catholic Church.

Back in Löderup, we lived in a three-story house—a quite wacky building that needed more work. Our address was Stinsgatan 8, where I spent the next five years of my life.

My father was a chief officer for a shipping company and worked across multiple gigantic vessels for DFDS, while my mother worked as a prison warden in Ystad. My father's occupation meant that he travelled frequently with work and thus was absent from our household quite a lot. Physically, my father wasn't there so often. That's why he made the times he was close to us children—me at the very least—matter so much. He was, to me, a good father despite not being present so often, and I have a lot of good memories of him.

From my perspective, I was part of a very healthy family—perhaps that was bliss or a mindset built with toys and gadgets, which I wasn't a stranger to receiving. I remember the birthday of my sister, Beatrice, and how I, ME, received a Digimon toy from our parents on HER birthday!

I don't remember who exactly it was from, but it was most likely our mother, as our father worked very much during his time in Löderup. Whoops! Spoilers! "His time in Löderup" doesn't that imply that he eventually moves out of Löderup? One step at a time! Back in line, please.

We used to have chickens and hens living in our garden—they had their own hen house and produced eggs for us. They were, however, obsessed with our downstairs living room and were watching television together with us! Sitting on the TV, on the sofa, or anywhere as long as they could be close to the TV apparatus. Now in hindsight, they might simply have been afraid of being outside due to the lost hen—we had a hen that suddenly disappeared from our family. I vaguely remember a legend about the black hen—it was so majestic that it simply could repel any attackers and safeguard the rest of the pack from the mysterious fox roaming around in the countryside!

It truly was peaceful times in Löderup, although my oldest brother Christian moved out of the household during 2003, if I understand/remember everything correctly. He eventually left Sweden to enrol in the French Foreign Legion. He took a win-loss gamble, one that my father has spoken highly about, seeing as he wasn't guaranteed success by travelling to France. I can vividly remember a nightmare of trying to climb the staircase up towards Christian's room on the third floor whilst the step that I put my foot on fell towards a bottomless black pit alongside the steps above it. It made me too afraid to visit my brother on the top floor; it was the only section of the house that I stopped visiting. Although I can remember visiting his room at some point to see all of his painted Warhammer figures. I always found them cool.

Our family had a neighbouring family, the Beraz family, consisting of Robert, Leah, and their son Sebastian. Sebastian was the same age as Carl-Philip, and we all used to play together. Sometimes we climbed trees at our place or jumped on the trampoline at theirs. We also often ran around the plains and forests with sticks, pretending to shoot each other.

At that time, Sebastian wasn't just our best friend; he was our only friend in Löderup. We spent time with each other every single day. Robert, a carpenter who also dabbled in smithing, would produce toys for us like shurikens, and one time, he even made a crossbow. Oh, and all the times we had water balloon wars were amazing!

When I was around 7 years old, during 2005, my mother and father split up and filed for divorce. My mother received sole custody of us, the four remaining children, and moved to Ystad together with us, taking upon herself the role of the sole parent for us children. She worked tirelessly in order to provide a good life for us— something that she was able to do, seeing as I never needed anything. I received toys, a Nintendo DS, although she was kind of a cheapskate when it came to clothes and would only buy clothes second-hand through Blocket and Tradera.*

We wore brands like Armani, Lacoste, Dolce & Gabbana, and other designer labels but at just a fraction of the cost. My mom was incredibly resourceful and thrifty, which she had to be as a single mother raising four children on her own. Her keen sense of economy didn't just help us look good without breaking the bank; it taught me early on about making the most out of limited resources. She somehow managed to provide for us while still letting us enjoy a few luxuries here and there, always balancing practicality with style.

*Blocket is a Swedish site for buying and selling items, while Tradera is an auction site for second-hand goods.

For now, let's get back into the subject and jump upon the common thread. We have talked about:

- My family
- My acting career, starting as a baby
- My upbringing in Löderup

And now we are getting started on the first chapter! My life in Ystad, internationally known as Y-Town.

Östra Skolan (Year 2003 - 2009)

Preschool (Year 2003)

I enrolled in "Östra Skolan" at the age of 7, and before I realised it, I started helping out the other children with their homework except this one kid, Yassir Fathullah, with whom I wound up having math competitions to see who could finish the next chapters of our math book the quickest. I remember that his mother was a teacher and that he received a lot of help at home—eventually, I gave up on studying at his pace as he really stepped up and it was hard to follow in his footsteps. Now, in hindsight, of course, I wish that I continued the race with him and studied at his pace. He grew up to be a very intellectual man with an impressive degree—if I didn't choose to enrol in crime, I could have lived his life.

I had the potential to be a proper scholar, at the very least, judging from my merits from elementary school.

Another interesting character from my days at Östra was Kevin Ekberg—a lovely lad from Ecuador who migrated with his family after his first year in kindergarten in the States, giving him an extra year of education before he even arrived at our school in time for kindergarten. I loved spending time with him—I remember that we were the only two that could speak English at that point, he from his year enrolled in a school in the States and me from my obsessive gaming disorder. I played a lot of Runescape with my brothers (Carl-Philip and Carl-Axel) and friends of our family, the Serlstedt family. Ekberg and I even got told at some point that we weren't allowed to speak any more English at school because it was keeping the other kids out of our conversations!
How absurd not being allowed to speak English at school.

During my time at Östra Skolan, I had a solid group of friends and would actually consider myself pretty popular. I was lucky enough to have a range of different friends, each bringing their own interests and quirks to the mix. Some friends shared my enthusiasm for sports, while others were my go-to group for things like gaming, music, or just hanging out and having a laugh. Having a varied social circle helped me feel connected to different sides of myself, and it gave me a sense of belonging that I hadn't really experienced before. Those friendships taught me a lot about loyalty, shared experiences, and finding common ground, even among very different personalities.

I used to play a lot of soccer together with a few of my classmates and the rest of the school. Essentially every break until my addiction kicked in and I reprioritised.

More of my addiction is to come.

Grade 2 (Year 2006)

I decided to start programming a web browser using Visual Studio Basics Portable at the age of 7. With the vast ocean of tutorials available online, I figured it was the perfect opportunity to combine learning with creating something usable.

It began with setting up the development environment and understanding how to create a basic GUI. I followed tutorials that taught me how to integrate a basic WebBrowser control to render websites.

As I dove deeper, I explored adding essential features like:

- **Navigation Buttons:** Forward, Backward, Refresh, and Stop.
- **URL Bar:** Allowing users to type in web addresses.
- **Basic Settings:** Options like setting a homepage or clearing browsing data.

Each feature was a small victory, fueling my excitement to learn more.

Grade 3 (Year 2007)

One of the most vivid memories I have from Östra Skolan involved my brother Carl-Axel and a schoolmate named Karl-Johan Wallander. It all went down one afternoon next to Saltsjöbaden in Ystad, on a playground that, on any other day, was a place of laughter and play.

That day, however, the playground became the setting for a confrontation that none of us would forget. The tension between Karl-Johan and Carl-Axel had been brewing for weeks. Whether it was a clash of egos or a misunderstanding that had escalated beyond repair, it all came to a head at that moment.

I remember watching from a distance as the argument between them grew more heated. Words were exchanged, and then suddenly, Karl-Johan threw the first punch. Without thinking, I rushed towards them. My instinct was to protect my brother at all costs.

Carl-Axel staggered back, trying to fend off Karl-Johan's blows. Seeing my brother in trouble ignited a surge of adrenaline in me. I leapt onto Karl-Johan's back, wrapping my arms around his neck in a desperate attempt to pull him off Carl-Axel. The world around us blurred into a cacophony of shouts and the distant sounds of kids playing, oblivious to the scuffle.

Karl-Johan thrashed wildly, trying to shake me off. I held on as tightly as I could, my grip fueled by a mix of fear and determination. My heart pounded in my chest, the rush of the fight making time seem to slow down. It felt like an eternity, but in reality, it was only a few chaotic moments before a teacher noticed the commotion and rushed over to break it up.

We were pulled apart, each of us panting and flushed with the heat of the confrontation. The teacher's stern face loomed over us as she demanded an explanation. I stood there, catching my breath, feeling a mix of pride for defending my brother and anxiety about the trouble we were sure to face.

That fight with Karl-Johan was more than just a playground scuffle. It was a moment that cemented my loyalty to my brother and showed me the lengths I was willing to go to protect my family. Even though the consequences were severe—we both ended up in the principal's office and our parents were called—I couldn't help but feel a sense of solidarity with Carl-Axel.

As we sat side by side in the principal's office, waiting for our parents to arrive, Carl-Axel turned to me and gave a small nod of gratitude. It was in that silent acknowledgement that I realised the depth of our bond, one that would carry us through many more challenges in the years to come.

Grade 4 (Year 2008)

During the year of 2008, I heard some of the older people in school, Alessandro Crnomat (later to be known as Juden), Ashab Alliberg, and Nick Serlstedt, talk about a card game called "Magic: The Gathering" that could be played locally at "Legacy Games," a store located on the main square of Ystad—a 2-minute walk from my apartment. One day, at the age of 9, I decided to be a part of this majestic game and thus I summoned my spirits and went inside "Legacy Games" and presented myself in front of three different individuals—Fab, Anders Hektor, and Johan Hägerhult. After having presented myself, Fab, as I like to call him, simply said: "No, you're not a William— you are a Hugo!" With those few words, my entire life changed.

I instantly got addicted to Magic: The Gathering— referred to as "Cardboard Crack." I began playing it at home with my older brother Carl-Axel, at school with Axel Larsson and Nick Serlstedt, and at Legacy Games with Fab, Johan, and some other blokes.

On my birthday one day, I received 500 SEK, and I went straight to the card store to blow it all on Magic booster packs together with Alessandro Crnomat, ripping up one after the other for 15 unique cards of the set "Shards of Alara". We paid 35 crowns per package and competed to see who could pull the best cards. Eventually, Alessandro pulled a foil Tezzeret the Seeker, a card that today would be worth almost 500 SEK. My mom yelled at me for "wasting" all my money at once. To this day, I regret not choosing the pack with Alessandro's foil, Tezzeret.

A memory from when I was around 9 years old. It was a time when I frequently visited Legacy Games, my local game store. The older players, around 15 years old, had just finished a draft and had accumulated a lot of Magic: The Gathering cards. These cards, often deemed "bulk-cards," held no significant value to seasoned players.

One player, named Hector, had a pile of at least 45 cards that he no longer needed. He handed the stack to me without a second thought. I was completely baffled by his generosity.

"Are you really giving this pile to me?" I asked, still in disbelief.

"Yes," Hector replied simply.

"I don't believe you. What happens if I throw it in the trash?" I questioned, trying to grasp the reality of receiving so many free cards.

"Well, then you throw away your brand new cards," he said with a shrug.

I remember clutching those cards, feeling an overwhelming sense of gratitude and excitement. For a young player like me, this was a treasure trove. Those cards, though deemed worthless by experienced players, were a goldmine to me. It wasn't just about the cards themselves but the kindness of someone sharing their passion and resources with a newcomer. It was moments like these that deepened my love for the game and the community around it.

I visited my father's place in Löderup every now and then when he was home from his work at sea. During those periods, I normally spent time with Sebastian as well. I even managed to get him hooked on the same hobby as me: Magic the Gathering!

We used to play Magic together, along with computer games like Counter-Strike. Those times were some of the best moments of my childhood, bonding over shared interests and enjoying each other's company.

During that period, one of the most unforgettable experiences was our trip to Disneyland Paris. Axel Larsson, one of my best friends at the time, had a father who often arranged family vacations and outings. This time, he managed to organise an incredible trip for our class to Paris, inviting everyone for a small fee. It was a rare opportunity, and we were all thrilled.

The anticipation built up for weeks before the trip. Our class was buzzing with excitement, and we talked endlessly about which rides we wanted to go on and which Disney characters we hoped to meet. The journey to Paris felt like an adventure in itself, filled with laughter and camaraderie.

Once we arrived, Disneyland was everything we had imagined and more. The magic of the place was palpable, and we were instantly transported to a world of fairy tales and fantasies. We explored the park together, hopping from ride to ride. We screamed our hearts out on Space Mountain, laughed on It's a Small World, and marvelled at the enchanting parades and fireworks that lit up the night sky.

One of the highlights was meeting our favourite Disney characters. We took countless photos, our faces beaming with joy. The entire class bonded over shared experiences, and it felt like we were part of one big, happy family. Axel's father had truly outdone himself, and we were all grateful for his generosity.

Apart from the Disneyland trip, my everyday life was closely intertwined with the Larsson family. I practically lived at their place, spending most of my free time with Axel and his older brother, André. The Larssons were warm and welcoming, and their home became my second home.

Axel and I shared countless adventures together, from playing video games late into the night to exploring the skate-park by the woods near their place. André, being older, often joined us and added an extra layer of fun and mischief to our activities. Their family dog, Dixi, was always part of the action. We affectionately called him Diski (as he often licked the plates clean before they went into the dishwasher).

These moments were filled with laughter and a sense of belonging. The Larsson household was a place where I could be myself, surrounded by friends who felt more like family. Little did I know that these cherished memories would lay the foundation for the friendships and experiences that would shape my life in the years to come.

And a year or two later we actually went to Tropical Island in Berlin together with the Larsson family and classmates.

Grade 5 (Year 2009)

In 2010, when I was 11 years old, my big brother Carl-Axel bought me Pokemon SoulSilver for Nintendo DS and it was practically the nicest thing anyone had ever done for me. I truly treasured it and was playing consistently.

There are countless memories from that time, each one adding a unique layer to my story. One such memory was our trip to Tropical Islands in Berlin, another incredible adventure arranged by Axel's father.

Tropical Islands was a massive indoor water park and resort, boasting a tropical climate all year round. It was a place where you could escape the cold and grey of a European winter and immerse yourself in a lush, warm paradise. The excitement we felt as we boarded the bus for Berlin was palpable. We could hardly contain our anticipation, chattering non-stop about the fun that awaited us.

Upon arrival, we were awestruck by the sheer scale of the place. It was like stepping into a different world. Palm trees, sandy beaches, and turquoise waters stretched out before us, all under a giant dome that seemed to touch the sky. The air was filled with the sounds of laughter, splashing water, and tropical birds, creating an atmosphere of perpetual summer.

We wasted no time diving into the activities. The water slides were a big hit, and we spent hours racing each other down the twisting, turning chutes. The wave pool was another favourite, where we pretended to surf the rolling waves. There were also quieter moments, lounging on the beach, building sandcastles, and floating lazily down the lazy river.

One of the highlights was exploring the rainforest area. It was a sprawling, lush section of the park filled with exotic plants and animals. We wandered through the winding paths, marvelling at the beauty and serenity of the place. It was easy to forget that we were inside a massive dome, as the environment felt so authentic.

Evenings at Tropical Islands were magical. The park was beautifully lit, and we would gather for dinner at one of the many restaurants, sharing stories and laughter over delicious meals. The sense of camaraderie was strong, and these moments of togetherness were some of the most memorable parts of the trip.

My bond with the Larsson family deepened during this time. Axel, André, and I were practically inseparable, and their father treated me like one of their own. This sense of belonging was invaluable, especially during the tumultuous years of adolescence.

Reflecting on these experiences, it's clear that these trips and adventures were more than just fun getaways. They were formative experiences that shaped my outlook on life, my friendships, and my understanding of what it meant to be part of a community. Whether it was the magic of Disneyland or the tropical paradise in Berlin, each adventure added a new chapter to the story of my life, filled with joy, laughter, and the warmth of friendship.

I truly recommend you visit Tropical Island; it's a really beautiful place. If you are currently reading this and are located in Europe, that is.

By the time I turned 10, I began to understand just how much effort my mom put into taking care of us and managing the household. She worked tirelessly to ensure that our fridge was always stocked with home-cooked food so that we could have a warm meal even when she was away at work. Despite carrying over a million

Swedish crowns in debt and not receiving any child support from our father, she somehow managed to put food on the table and even afford designer clothes for us kids. Looking back, it amazes me how she stretched every crown to give us a stable and comfortable life, all while shouldering the financial weight alone. Her resilience and dedication left a lasting impact on me.

When 5th grade ended, it was time for 6th grade. For most of the class, nothing changed since classes remained in the same school. However, for me, Bärnheim, Ekberg, Omran, and others, it marked a significant shift as we transferred to Kunskapsskolan of Ystad.

Kunskapsskolan: (Year 2010 - 2014)

Kunskapsskolan was a place full of distractions and opportunities. There, I experienced my first love, discovered cannabis, and delved into a seminar on narcotics led by our math teacher, Mimmi. This seminar sparked my interest in researching actual information about different substances, particularly cannabis. It was also where I began playing League of Legends, a game I would continue to play for years until 2016.

Grade 6 (Year 2010)

At the beginning of my time in Kunskapsskolan, at the age of 12 ½ or, rounded up at 13—I met so many new faces, but one face in particular stood out. Bengt Hansson—my childhood acquaintance who was the best of friends with my father. He was a mathematical genius and was one of the teachers at Kunskapsskolan. I used to visit his place and play with his dog called Melody! He is an incredibly kind soul and I appreciated spending time around him and would like to thank him for teaching me maths alongside my other maths teacher, Mathias Ljunggren.

I was still spending regular time with Fab, the Magic player from way back when I was a little child, and I stuttered every single word I tried to pronounce. But we still played Magic!

Although... Legacy Games did, in fact, close down. Despite Alessandro's enormous motivation to succeed in Sweden, being an Italian immigrant, he wasn't a budgeting genius. Unfortunately, he failed by taking advice from others (no names mentioned, cough, you're in the book, cough) and was convinced to spend a large proportion of his budget on board games instead of Magic, which actually sold and was played all day long! As a result, he ended up with boxes of cardboard games that no one played.

Well, I am getting a bit off-topic. I was just incredibly sad when Legacy Games closed. However, luckily for me, Fab opened up "The Community" in a basement venue he rented from the property manager in Västra Sjöstaden, where he lived with his parents.

Aaaaand! Anders Larsson, the father of Axel and André, began selling underwear to the store that opened up in place of Legacy Games.

The new location never quite captured the magic and camaraderie of Legacy Games, but "The Community" became a new haven for our gatherings. It was a place where we could continue our shared passion for Magic and spend time with friends. Despite the setback with the store, Fab's perseverance and dedication created a space where we could still come together and enjoy the game we loved. So luckily I still had that going for me.

Grade 7 (Year 2011)

I started playing Magic a lot more often, and when I began my relationship with Gloria (my first girlfriend). We received a bus card from Samir Arabi-Eter to help us travel to Malmö to play Magic. In Malmö, I met many competitive players who helped me in my journey to become a better Magic: The Gathering player. The first time I met Samir, he was wearing a Blitzcrank hoodie from League of Legends, which was a great conversation starter for us to get talking.

So many things were going on simultaneously while I was studying at Kunskapsskolan. Magic, League of Legends, cannabis, love (Gloria), the beginning of my criminal 'career,' trouble at home, and such. I had difficulties studying at school since we were responsible for our own assignments and didn't have to spend time in actual classes. We simply had a meeting at the beginning of the "school day" and a meeting at the end of the "school day." Most of the time, I spent playing on the monstrous ASUS Republic of Gamers laptop that my mother bought for me—it cost her 12,000 SEK. Surely half a month's pay for my mom. She must have loved me a lot.

At this time, when I attended Kunskapsskolan, I used to go to LAN parties at my cousin's place and play League of Legends with Axel Wiberg and Johannes. Johannes' parents, Marie Larsson and Johan Larsson, had this fantastic place in Lindby, which looked almost like a tourist resort abroad with a swimming pool and everything.

Where does Hatake even originate from? Well, it's the surname of my favourite character from the Japanese animated TV series Naruto, created by Masashi Kishimoto.

Because my mother worked as a prison warden and wanted to protect our family's integrity, she didn't allow us to use our real names when registering for social media like Facebook. So, I adopted my nickname Hugo, given to me by Fab, and combined it with the surname Hatake from one of my favourite TV series. In Japanese culture, surnames traditionally come before first names, so Ernst-William Hertz would become Hertz Ernst-William. Thus, Hatake Hugo was born.

I feel like we're skipping forward and backwards continuously in the chronological order of my life.

Grade 8 (Year 2012)

2012 was a sad year, the year that my uncle unfortunately took his own life. The great Russian teacher and translator who was called Hans Hertz. We used to call him Farbror Hasse.

My first time smoking cannabis was with Qlino and Mackan. We sat together on a bench at Ardenner when I was 14. After coughing a lot, I realised that my entire perception of the environment had changed. It was an incredibly uplifting experience, and from that point on, I was hooked. The only reason I was able to join them for a smoke in the first place was by pretending that I had already smoked cannabis before.

I remember messaging Qlino on Facebook Messenger, asking if he could sell me some weed. At first, he refused to acknowledge what I was talking about and insisted that he didn't understand. Determined, I lied and said that I also smoked but was currently out. Eventually, he let me know that I could meet him after school.

That first encounter with cannabis opened up a new world for me. It wasn't just about the high; it was the sense of camaraderie and belonging that came with it. From that day, I began to see the world differently, and my journey into the world of cannabis had officially begun.

Qlino was, however, not a dealer and just used to occasionally smoke cannabis. I needed to find a dealer and when I one day was walking towards the train station together with a good friend of mine, Lennie Blixt, and we saw a guy in front of us and Lennie was telling me.

"That guy sells weed."

I was like, "No way"

"Go forth and ask him and you will see," Lennie convinced me.

Hence I did, I got to meet Saddaka who opened up his jacket pocket and brought forth a huge zip bag in the middle of the street with a lot of smaller zip bags filled with "slangs" of hashish. We were stunned!

A slang, when used in relation to hash, is a term for 100-crowns worth of smoke. It ranges from 0.6 to 1.0 grams depending on where you live and what dealers originate there. Saddaka used to sell us 0.8 grams per 100 crowns. He was a student at the neighbouring school, right next to Kunskapsskolan, but I had never seen him before. We just found ourselves a dealer and started buying from him on a regular basis.

My cousin (from my father's side) Johannes Larsson used to hustle together the 100 crowns that we needed in order to buy a "slang" of hashish when we were 14 years old. He ran around the cafeteria, begging people for 5 crowns here, 10 crowns there, and so forth until it was enough to go and exchange the money for a crisp 100 crown bill at Ica. He was a hard-working man, my cousin.

Cannabis became my escape, my secret companion that helped me deal with the pressures of school, family, and my burgeoning identity.

But with this new hobby came the need for a steady supply. My small allowance couldn't sustain my growing habit. That's when the idea hit me—why not become the supplier? I had the connections, and there was a demand among my peers.

Word spread quickly, and soon I was known as the guy who could hook you up. The thrill of making money, combined with the respect and fear I commanded, was intoxicating. It felt like I had found my calling. I was careful, though—discreet transactions, always watching my back, never talking to strangers about my side hustle.

Balancing school, my relationship with Gloria, and my burgeoning business was challenging. There were close calls, like the time a teacher almost caught me making a deal in the bathroom. But the adrenaline rush of those moments only fueled my determination. I was good at this, and for the first time in my life, I felt in control.

However, the path I chose was fraught with danger. I started to realise that the more successful I became, the more risks I had to take. The money was good, but it came with a price later known as stress.

This was the beginning of my journey into a world that was both exhilarating and perilous. It was a path that would shape my future in ways I couldn't yet imagine. But at that moment, as a fourteen-year-old kid in Ystad, all I cared about was the next deal, the next high, and the feeling of invincibility that came with being Hatake Hugo.

However my business sense quickly kicked in and I realised that instead of being solely a consumer I realised that I could provide it to others as well.

Playing League of Legends with my friends in the study rooms was memorable, despite its distraction from studying. I recall a moment when Hannes Strömberg joked about how he smokes weed and jokingly said that we should go for a smoke. Lennie Blixt and I replied, "Sure, let's go and smoke."

We rolled a joint and smoked it, leaving Hannes astonished at what he witnessed. That was the beginning of my friendship with Hannes—and also the beginning of his cannabis consumption, which Marie-Ann, Gloria's mother, kept asking us about if we knew something.

One particular friend that stands out from my time at Kunskapsskolan is Tuva Tuenter. Tuva had the most beautiful laughter, and I truly believe she was my best friend during this period. One vivid memory I have with her is when we went for a stroll around the area near our school. During this walk, I explained to her in detail how I planned to slowly spread cannabis around to increase its demand after people developed an interest in it. Her support and understanding during our conversations meant a lot to me.

I had always heard that my brother, Calle, was into the business of selling cannabis and I eventually talked to my brother about wanting to earn together 12 000 SEK in order to buy some Magic cards.

I came up with the proposition to start selling cannabis with a couple of friends and they thought it was cool. They wanted in, so when I got my first slab (100 grams) of hash for 6000 crowns on credit from Calle, I cut it into four pieces of 25 grams each and provided it to four of my friends, asking them for 2000 crowns each. This yielded a profit of 2000 crowns in about 10 days.

When my partners, Sammy Bolin, Ragnar Vanheden, Rähli and Charles Ingvar, had finished selling their parts of the slab and left me the funds, I gave Calle his 6000 crowns and kept the 2000 in profit.

This gave me a sort of rush—realising that I could sell cannabis and make a profit from the drug that I began to love consuming. This was at the age of 15. Who could have known that the clientele in the age range of 14-15 in Ystad, of all the places, would be so huge?

Bringing forth 2000 crowns in profit every 7-10 days meant a monthly profit of 6-8k at the age of 15 with minimum effort, a passive income. If that isn't impressive then I don't know what is.

I keep asking myself what this book ought to be about. Is it my relationships? My addictions? The following rap?

Verse 1: Locked up in this ward, mind spinning out of control,
They got me in a cage, but I'm still fighting for my soul,
Murder charge, pierced his throat, trying to survive,
He came at me first, but now I'm buried alive.

I remember that night, the darkness in his eyes,
Had to make a choice, or face my own demise,

Kept my mouth shut, didn't speak my truth,
Now I'm paying the price, locked away in my youth.

Chorus: Locked up, locked down, in this psychiatric town,
Fighting shadows in my mind, will I ever get out?
Locked up, locked down, trying to break these chains,
In this endless nightmare, can't escape the pain.

Verse 2: Doctors and nurses, they try to understand,
But they don't see the blood that's still on my hands,
They label me a danger, they say I lost control,
But deep inside I'm screaming, I just want to be whole.

Flashing lights, cold nights, locked in isolation,
Facing my demons, lost in contemplation,
They say I need help, but who's helping me?
In this maze of madness, will I ever be free?

Chorus: Locked up, locked down, in this psychiatric town,
Fighting shadows in my mind, will I ever get out?
Locked up, locked down, trying to break these chains,
In this endless nightmare, can't escape the pain.

Bridge: Memories haunt me, like ghosts in the night,
I see his face, I feel the fright,
The guilt and the rage, tearing me apart,
In this prison of my mind, where do I start?

Verse 3: Courtroom drama, kept my mouth shut tight,
Self-defense or not, they took away my light,
Now I'm living in this hell, surrounded by the lost,
Paying for my silence, but at what cost?
I'm more than a number, I'm more than this pain,
I'm a fighter, a survivor, breaking these chains,
One day I'll rise, from the ashes of this fight,
Find my redemption, step back into the light.

Chorus: Locked up, locked down, in this psychiatric town,
Fighting shadows in my mind, will I ever get out?
Locked up, locked down, trying to break these chains,
In this endless nightmare, can't escape the pain.

Outro: So here's my story, raw and unfiltered,
A tale of survival, in a world that's off-kilter,
Locked up but not broken, I'll find my way,
In this rap of life, I'll fight another day.

Spoiler-alert:

I am currently in a psychiatric ward due to a murder charge, which you now, in hindsight, obviously can see from both the title of the book and the cover.

As I sit here in the psychiatric ward, I often find myself reflecting on the choices I've made and the paths I've taken. The murder charge weighs heavily on my mind, a constant reminder of the consequences of my actions. It's a surreal experience, being in a place designed to heal the mind while grappling with the darkness within my own.

Writing this book, composing rap lyrics, and reflecting on my experiences have been therapeutic. Creativity has become my lifeline, a way to process my emotions and make sense of my past. It's through these creative outlets that I hope to connect with others and maybe, just maybe, help someone avoid the same mistakes I made.

I realise there are many aspects of my story that I haven't fully explored. For instance, the day my parents split up, how it felt to watch my family change overnight, or the first time I realised I had a knack for understanding people's desires and fears. These are the moments that shaped me, and they deserve to be told.

The day my parents divorced marked the end of an era and the beginning of a new, uncertain chapter. My mother's strength and resilience were a source of inspiration, but they also meant that I had to grow up faster than I was ready for. Looking back, I see how this pivotal moment pushed me toward seeking control in other areas of my life.

Despite the darkness, I still hold onto hope. I dream of a future where I can use my experiences to help others, to prevent someone else from falling into the same traps. I want to speak out about the dangers of substance abuse, the allure of easy money, and the importance of making the right choices.

Redemption is a long road, but I believe it's possible. Writing this book is a step in that direction. It's a way to confront my past, acknowledge my mistakes, and begin the process of healing. I hope that by sharing my story, I can inspire others to seek help and make positive changes in their lives.

Life is a complex journey filled with highs and lows, successes and failures. My story is just one of many, but it's a story worth telling. As I continue to write, I hope to uncover more truths about myself and the world around me. This book is not just about my past; it's about my present and my future, and the belief that no matter how far you've fallen, there's always a way back up

Back to my school years:

Being with Gloria during Kunskapsskolan was transformative. We met during one of those self-paced learning sessions at Kunskapsskolan, where I noticed her working diligently on a project. She had this aura of calm and focus that drew me in. One of our first conversations was about our favourite movies and series. She really enjoyed Twilight and that show with a woman living with guys, I believe it to be called New Girl. Gloria taught me the value of patience and understanding, qualities I desperately needed amidst the chaos of my life. I remember going for a walk with Pommac Skog Sundberg at Norra Promenaden in Ystad, accompanied by our family dog, a Shetland Sheepdog named Bobby. It was a peaceful afternoon, with the sun casting a golden hue over the landscape. As we strolled along the path, I spotted someone jogging on the other side of the river. It was Gloria. That was one of the first times I truly paid attention to her.

She was effortlessly graceful, her long black hair swinging with each stride, and she exuded an aura of determination. Our eyes met briefly, and I felt a strange mix of curiosity and admiration. Little did I know, this encounter would mark the beginning of something profound in my life. Back at Kunskapsskolan, we started chatting more frequently. We often found ourselves in the dining room, talking about everything from schoolwork to our dreams and fears. Pommac was usually with us, adding his own quirky humour to our conversations. These interactions made me realise how different Gloria was from anyone I had ever met. She was insightful, kind-hearted, and had an infectious enthusiasm for life. We began to take strolls around our neighbourhood, often accompanied by Bobby. These walks became a cherished routine. We talked about our favourite movies, shared funny stories from our childhoods, and sometimes just enjoyed the comfortable silence between us. Each walk deepened my feelings for her. She had this way of making the world seem brighter, more hopeful. I also do remember her negative attitude towards me insisting on us listening to music through my mobile speaker whilst going for a stroll, haha. She truly deemed me as a phoney for doing that.

One evening, as we walked under the fading light of a setting sun, I realised how much I truly cared for her. Gloria was out of this world, or at least that's how I remember it now. She brought a sense of stability and warmth to my otherwise chaotic life.

Despite the tumultuous path I was on with my growing involvement in dealing and the pressures of school, Gloria remained a constant source of support. She was my anchor, the one person who saw beyond my tough exterior and believed in the goodness within me. Our relationship was not without its challenges, but the bond we shared was strong enough to weather any storm.

As I look back on those days, I can see how vital Gloria was in shaping my journey. She taught me the value of genuine connection and showed me a glimpse of the life I could have if I chose a different path. Her influence continues to be a guiding light in my memories, a reminder of the love and hope that once filled my heart.

Cannabis was more than just a way to unwind; it became a crutch. The first time I smoked with Qlino and Mackan was a revelation. The haze of smoke clouded my reality, making everything seem distant and manageable. But with each high came a new low, a deeper need to escape. My involvement in selling began as a way to fund my habit, but it quickly spiralled into something much larger and more dangerous.

When I started selling cannabis, it felt like a natural extension of my newfound identity. My brother Calle provided my first slab, and from there, I learned the ropes of dealing. The thrill of making money and the respect it commanded was addictive. I vividly remember the first time I handed over a piece of hash to a friend and pocketed the cash. It felt like power, but it also marked the beginning of a path I couldn't easily turn back from. The transition from a curious and imaginative child to a teenager entangled in the world of crime was gradual, almost imperceptible. It began with small, seemingly inconsequential decisions that snowballed into a lifestyle I couldn't easily escape.

Growing up, the absence of my father loomed large over our household. His sporadic appearances and subsequent disappearances left a void that I desperately tried to fill. My brother, always looking for a way out of the same oppressive environment, turned to the French Foreign Legion. His departure was a stark reminder of our fractured family and the lengths we were willing to go to escape our realities.

At some point, I travelled with my cousin to Lorensborg, Malmö, to meet a drug dealer named Leffe. I requested a slab of 100 grams of hash on a week's credit. Leffe, a cool bloke, asked my cousin if I could really get rid of a slab in a week. My cousin confidently replied, "Yeah, if Hugo says he can get rid of it in a week, then he can."

I believe I was 15 at that point, and my cousin Johannes was 14. I had already been taking hash on credit from my brother but wanted a higher supply at once, so I sought an alternative source to juggle in between. I sold this slab independently, as Sammy, Ragnar Vanheden, and

Charles Ingvar were already hustling from the other slab. I sold any given amount for 100 crowns each to a different clientele than my "crew."

We didn't compete with each other, but there was, however, a friendly rivalry over who could sell the most. Charles usually won.

Left to my own devices, I began to seek out ways to assert control over my life. The streets of our neighbourhood, with their own set of rules and hierarchies, became both a refuge and a trap. I started small—running errands for the dealers in Malmö, handling hash transactions, and slowly gaining their trust. Each successful job brought a sense of accomplishment and a fleeting high that I quickly grew addicted to.

Dealing drugs became my primary occupation. The money was fast, and the thrill of evading law enforcement gave me a sense of invincibility. Yet, behind the facade of confidence, there was always an underlying fear—fear of getting caught, fear of the violence that surrounded the trade, and fear of losing myself completely to this dangerous game.

Despite the risks, there were moments of camaraderie and loyalty that provided a semblance of family. My crew and I shared not just the profits but also our dreams and fears. We were bound by a mutual understanding of our struggles and the lengths we would go to survive. However, this bond was fragile, easily shattered by betrayal and the constant pressure of the criminal underworld.

During this time, my passion for strategy and planning didn't wane; instead, it adapted to my new reality. I found myself applying the same meticulous attention to detail that I used in Magic: The Gathering to my illicit activities. Planning drug runs, managing supply chains, and outmanoeuvring rivals became a dark mirror of the games I once loved.

But the thrill of the game came at a high cost. The constant stress and the ever-present danger began to take a toll on my mental health. I started using drugs not just as a source of income but also as a way to numb the growing anxiety and depression. The line between dealer and user blurred, and I found myself spiralling deeper into the abyss.

During those months of uncertainty and tension, one of the few things that brought solace and joy into my life was my time with Gloria. She became my anchor, my escape from the harsh reality surrounding us. We spent countless hours lying in bed, wrapped in the soft glow of our shared sanctuary, watching anime together.

Our favourite series varied, but we both had a penchant for the classics as well as newer hits. "Hunter x Hunter" was one of our staples; we laughed and cried with the characters, discussing every plot twist and character development. Gloria's eyes would light up with excitement during battle scenes, and she had an incredible knack for predicting what would happen next.

On lazy afternoons, we'd switch to something more lighthearted like "My Neighbor Totoro". The whimsical worlds of Studio Ghibli were a perfect escape, and we'd often find ourselves lost in discussions about the intricacies of their animation and storytelling. Gloria had a keen eye for detail and could point out things I never would have noticed on my own.

When the days felt particularly heavy, we'd dive into the intricate plotlines of "Sword Art Online" or "Full Metal Alchemist," losing ourselves in the complexity of the narratives. These shows sparked endless debates between us, often stretching late into the night. Gloria always had an insightful perspective, and her intelligence shone through in our conversations.

Gloria's family was lively and unique in their own way. She had a rabbit named Zippy and two younger twin sisters named No and Nava. Interestingly, if either sister had been born alone, their name would have been

Navano—a playful twist that reflected the family's creativity. Gloria also had two older siblings, Joacim and Alexandra. The household, composed of No, Nava, Marie-Ann (their mother), Zippy, and Gloria herself, was full of life and warmth.

Marie-Ann raised her children as vegetarians, and no meat was ever served in their home. I often joined them for meals, and Marie-Ann's cooking was exceptional. Her pasta salad was legendary, a dish in a league of its own. However, I sometimes wonder if I influenced Gloria's dietary choices. I introduced her to chicken dishes from Pizzeria Triangeln, and over time, she seemed to drift away from the strict vegetarian path. It makes me smile now, thinking back—because today, I've embraced veganism myself. Life has a funny way of coming full circle.

Our bed became a haven of sorts. Surrounded by pillows and blankets, we'd curl up together, my head resting on her chest, listening to her every heartbeat. The rhythm of our breathing would sync as we watched episode after episode, finding comfort in each other's presence. The simple act of being together, sharing those moments, made the outside world fade away, if only temporarily.

Outside of our anime marathons, we'd often talk about our dreams and plans for the future. Gloria had a contagious optimism that made me believe that things could get better. She was passionate about becoming a YouTuber and even the idea of traveling to Europe someday, something we used to talk about with her mother. Buying interrail passes and simply jumping the train tracks! Her dreams became my dreams, and together, we imagined a life beyond the confines of our current situation.

We'd occasionally take breaks from our screen time to stroll through the neighbourhood, hand in hand. These walks were filled with easy conversation and quiet moments of reflection. Even the simplest outings felt special with Gloria by my side.

Our bond deepened with each passing day. The love and understanding we shared became a beacon of hope and stability in my otherwise tumultuous life. Gloria's unwavering support and companionship gave me strength, reminding me that no matter what challenges lay ahead, we could face them together.

Those days with Gloria were a reminder of the beauty of everyday moments and the profound impact of having someone who truly understands and stands by you. In a world filled with uncertainty, our time together was a sanctuary, a testament to the power of love and connection.

I still remember our first kiss vividly. We were sitting on her bed, along with Sarah Johansson. I had never kissed anyone before, and Gloria, noticing my nervousness, guided me through the process. She took good care of me, making sure I felt comfortable and cherished. That moment was the beginning of a profound connection between us.

I did, however, at some point break up with her due to my addiction to League of Legends, which started taking over my life. I spent more time gaming than I did with her, leading to arguments and misunderstandings. Eventually, this addiction caused us to break up. It was a tough lesson on the importance of balance and prioritising the people who matter most.

During my relationship with Gloria, I found out from a good friend of mine, Nikita, that she had been assaulted in the bathroom by Vincent. This revelation came as a shock. I encouraged her to report the incident to the principal and the police, which she did. This resulted in both of us being called into the police office, accompanied by my mother, to provide statements as witnesses.

Why do I bring this up? After I broke up with Gloria, she eventually started seeing Vincent. Despite our breakup, I still cared deeply for her, and this development made me extremely paranoid and concerned. My feelings for her were still strong, even though my passion for the game I played had driven a wedge between us.

I remember a specific visit to her place, sitting on her bed, trying to convince her to break up with Vincent. It was a complicated situation, driven by my lingering feelings and our shared history. In hindsight, it was a selfish move, but it demonstrated the depth of my emotions for her.

After our conversation, she left her apartment to meet Vincent in Rydsgård, a suburb of Ystad. When she returned, she relayed his parting words: "Can I at least jizz in your face one last time?" Hearing this infuriated me. The thought of her being treated so disrespectfully by someone I already had reasons to despise was too much to bear.

This period of my life was a tumultuous one, marked by conflicting emotions and difficult choices. It was a time when I had to navigate the complexities of love, jealousy, and protecting those I cared about, all while dealing with my own insecurities and shortcomings.

I just want to continue writing but sometimes I have to stop myself in order to really zoom out a little bit and try looking at this from the bigger picture. Who's my target audience? Is it intended for myself? Or for my father and mother? What convinced me to writing a book about my life? Perhaps this is a book that I could actually get published and utilise in order to generate a revenue stream.

At the very least, I know that you are reading this right now. That's the most important part. You are a very wholesome individual and I would like to thank you for reading this.

There was an evening when the children of the town got together and had a bonfire at Västervångsskolan. This was during a period when I wasn't with Gloria. I met a lovely lady there named Amanda. We ended up chatting a bit, and due to the cold, we even started sharing a glove while the other glove remained in the pocket.

Amanda and I hit it off immediately. Her warmth and friendliness made the chilly night feel much cosier. We talked about our interests, school, and life in general. The connection felt effortless, and I found myself drawn to her in a way that was both exciting and new. However, the "problem" was that she was together with Vårtan, a bloke from Simrishamn.

Vårtan got wind of us talking and called me a "Max-tramp," generalising me with the other teenagers who spent their time after school at the hamburger chain Max.

His words stung, not just because of the insult, but because they highlighted the barriers between Amanda and me. Despite this, Amanda and I continued to stay in touch.

There was a point where my mother grounded me by taking away both my phone and computer, leaving me with only my Nintendo Wii. She didn't understand that it could access the internet, which it could only do because I had modified the firmware by installing a "Homebrew" package. I wound up writing for hours with Amanda by pointing at the screen with the remote and pressing one letter at a time. It took forever compared to her typing speed, but I was in love to the point where nothing could keep me from staying in touch with her.

Our conversations over the Wii were filled with youthful exuberance and a touch of rebellion. I remember the late-night chats, where we'd talk about our dreams, our favourite movies, and the music we loved. Amanda had a knack for making me laugh, even through the slow, cumbersome process of typing out messages on the Wii. If only she hadn't been together with that darn Vårtan. The knowledge that she was with Vårtan always lingered in the back of my mind, a constant reminder that our connection had its limits. Despite this, I cherished every moment we shared, even if it was just through a screen. The way we managed to stay connected, despite the obstacles, made our bond feel even more special.

In hindsight, those conversations with Amanda were a beacon of light during a challenging time. They were filled with the kind of innocent, hopeful longing that only young love can bring. And even though we couldn't be together, those memories have stayed with me, a reminder of a time when love felt pure and boundless, and nothing could keep us apart.

Grade 9 (Year 2013 - 14)

Fab, being a Photoshop expert, helped me in my Art class by illustrating a picture of me where I was split into two people. On the one side, I had a devil horn and on the other side, I had a halo. Moa Gertsson gave me an A, and the picture got hung up outside our art-study room. Björn Neuhaser laughed and said that everyone knew that it was Fab that done the job for me.

We occasionally took trips to Gamleby with our school, and one particular moment sticks out. Those trips to Gamleby were a break from the usual routine, and somehow this one felt even more significant. The sewing class was like an island of calm—machines whirring softly, classmates focused on their work, and Moa right beside me. There was an odd comfort in it all, a sense of connection without words.

As I read through that final chapter of *Naruto*, each panel felt like a farewell. I'd followed these characters for years, seen them grow, struggle, and overcome. And now, here I was, on a simple school trip, experiencing the end of something that had been a huge part of my life. I felt a pang of sadness, but also a strange sense of closure.

Moa noticed my reaction, her quiet glance saying more than words could. She didn't need to ask, didn't need to say anything—her presence was enough. We shared that moment, surrounded by the steady rhythm of sewing machines and the warmth of our small group. In that silent understanding, it felt like a chapter of my own life was closing too, making space for something new.

Early adulthood (Age 16 - 20)

Österportsgymnasiet Year 2014 - 2017

School Year 1 (2014 - 15)

I do remember when I just got enrolled at Österportsgymnasiet and the new classmates appeared in front of me. There were some familiar faces, including people I was already involved with in the hash-selling business, and another face that I felt anxious about seeing.

For the first time ever, I actually got to meet Vårtan in person. The tension was palpable as our eyes met. All the stories and rumours about him flashed through my mind. I couldn't help but feel a mix of curiosity and apprehension.

Seeing him in the flesh was different from hearing about him through whispers and secondhand accounts. He carried himself with a certain confidence that was both intimidating and intriguing. I wondered how he would react to me, especially given our history with Amanda.

As we were introduced to each other, I felt a knot in my stomach. Despite my anxiety, I tried to keep a neutral demeanour. We exchanged a few words, and surprisingly, it wasn't as confrontational as I had feared. Perhaps the school setting and the presence of other classmates helped to diffuse any immediate tension.

Over time, I found myself observing Vårtan more closely. I wanted to understand the person behind the reputation. Despite my initial apprehension, I realised that he was just another student navigating the complexities of high school life, much like myself.

Our interactions remained civil, and while we were never close friends, we managed to coexist without any major conflicts. In a way, meeting him in person helped to demystify the image I had built up in my mind. It was a lesson in not letting preconceived notions dictate my perception of someone.

Reflecting on those early days at Österportsgymnasiet, I realise that the experience taught me a lot about facing my fears and keeping an open mind. Meeting Vårtan was a significant moment, marking the beginning of a new chapter in my life filled with unexpected encounters and personal growth.

I also met Charles Ingvar, Liam Schor and Loke Malmberg in my class, two homeboys who had previously attended Västervångsskolan and Norreportskolan. Charles went to the former school whilst Loke went to the latter. During my time in Ystad, there were three secondary schools: Norreportsskolan, Västervångsskolan, and Kunskapsskolan. As far as I know, there are probably still only three secondary schools there, even ten years later.

Charles and Loke were the best of friends and both of them were very cool. Charles had a great sense of humour, and Loke was always up for an adventure. They had this infectious energy that made every day exciting. Our class was called SA14B, and it was the best class I ever had in my entire life.

The bond we shared as a class was unparalleled. We supported each other through thick and thin, celebrated our successes together, and even managed to make the mundane moments memorable. Whether it was group projects, school trips, or just hanging out after school, we created memories that I still cherish to this day. The camaraderie and friendship in SA14B were truly special, and it played a significant role in shaping who I am today.

Kevin Ekberg was once again in my class, and he became one of my best friends throughout my journey.

Despite my involvement in the narcotics trade, I never pushed my agenda onto him. Kevin was a civilised, well-mannered, and very intelligent man. We shared a common goal of becoming police officers, which added an ironic twist to my life as a narcotics dealer.

Kevin's integrity and brilliance were evident in everything he did. He was dedicated to his studies and his dream of joining the police force. I admired his commitment and often found myself wishing I had the same level of dedication in my pursuits. Despite the path I chose, I always respected Kevin's choices and never tried to involve him in my illicit activities.

Looking back, it's a bit sad that I didn't involve him in my narcotic trade, not because I wanted him to partake in illegal activities, but because his intelligence and strategic thinking could have been invaluable. However, I am glad I didn't drag him into that world. Kevin deserved a future free from the complications and dangers of the narcotics trade.

If I could recommend anyone for any kind of occupation, it would be Kevin Ekberg. His brilliance, integrity, and dedication make him an exceptional individual. Our friendship was a bright spot in my tumultuous life, and I will always value the time we spent together.

I found myself once again back together with Gloria, and this time, with the maturity that came with age, I took on a more active role in their home. I occasionally helped Marie-Ann with giving the twins, No and Nava, their baths. The bathroom would fill with laughter as they splashed around, their giggles echoing through the house. I'd make silly faces to keep them entertained while Gloria handed me towels and soap. The steam from the warm water and the scent of their floral bubble bath created a cosy, comforting atmosphere. It was a simple act, but it made me feel like part of their family, sharing those little moments that held so much warmth.

After the baths, we'd wrap the twins in fluffy towels, and their tiny hands would reach for mine as I helped dry their hair. Sometimes, Gloria and I would sit with them afterward, telling bedtime stories and watching their eyes grow heavy with sleep. Being part of those quiet, tender moments gave me a sense of belonging that I cherished. The Engdahl home became more than just a place I visited; it felt like a second home where love was shared freely, even amid the busy chaos of everyday life.

There is one magical night that I will never forget-- well, at least, the main part. My memory is fogged from all the narcotics, brain-bleeding and PTSD, but this night stands out vividly. It was a night spent with Karla, Filip, Ragnar Vanheden and Charles Ingvar. We were around

16 years old and gathered in Fliip's parents' apartment. We had taken some substances and smoked a couple of hash joints on the balcony. Life felt perfect.

Suddenly, our dear comrade Charles suggested that we sit on the sofa. We did, and then he told us to close our eyes. We held them shut for three entire minutes. When Charles finally said, "OK! NOW YOU CAN OPEN THEM AGAIN.... Wiii," I opened my eyes to a breathtaking sight.

The entire living room was filled with candles, casting a warm and gentle glow. The light and warmth from the candles, combined with the camaraderie surrounding us, created an unforgettable atmosphere. It's been around 10 years since that night, but I still remember it perfectly. That moment is one of the many reasons why Charles Ingvar is one of my absolute favourite human beings on this planet.

In late October of 2014, from the 24th to the 26th, I found myself on a journey that combined my passion for Magic: The Gathering with the familiar thrill of competition. I packed my meticulously built black aggro deck, a relentless force designed to dominate the battlefield quickly, and set off from Ystad with a heart full of anticipation to Stockholm in order to take part of the annual Grand Prix tournament. The trip itself was almost a ritual, the train humming beneath me as I mentally rehearsed the strategy for my deck. Every card had a purpose, every move a plan.

Arriving at the tournament venue, the atmosphere buzzed with energy. The room was filled with seasoned players and newcomers alike in a total of 1043 players, each focused on their cards and the potential victories ahead. I found my place, laid out my deck, and took a moment to center myself. The matches began, and the room echoed with the soft shuffling of cards and the rustle of hushed conversations.

My first game was a testament to the power of my deck. I played swiftly, striking hard and fast, exploiting every weakness in my opponent's strategy. The tempo was relentless; my creatures hit the battlefield, pushing through with dark, shadowy force. The first victory was mine, a smooth and decisive win that sent a ripple of confidence through me.

The second match was a different kind of fight. My opponent, a seasoned player with a deck full of control spells, sought to stem the tide of my offense. But the black aggro deck I wielded was crafted for resilience and speed. With precise moves, I overwhelmed their defences, winning with a final blow that sealed my second victory.

It was during the third match that the day took a turn. My opponent was a young junior, wide-eyed and eager but prone to the small, understandable mistakes of inexperience. The game was intense; I felt the pressure of maintaining my winning streak. At a critical point, my opponent missed a trigger, a subtle but important detail that could shift the tide of battle. I paused, considering whether to let it pass. But fairness won over ambition. I gently corrected him, showing him the missed trigger and allowing him to resolve it.

This act of sportsmanship came at a cost. The corrected play turned the game on its head, shifting momentum in his favor. His deck came to life with renewed strength, and despite my best efforts, I found myself cornered. The final moments of the match were a blur of tapped lands and desperate plays, but the game slipped away. I lost the match, my winning streak broken.

The sting of defeat was softened by the respect I earned from those who witnessed the moment. The junior, grateful for my honesty, shook my hand with a wide grin. It was a reminder that Magic: The Gathering was not just about victories but about the shared love for the game, the lessons learned, and the camaraderie built across the table.

A shoutout goes to Matej Zatlkaj for winning the tournament.

As I packed up my deck, feeling the weight of both triumph and loss, I knew the journey from Ystad was worth every moment. It was a trip marked not only by competition but by the shared passion for strategy, fair play, and the stories that come from each match.

School Year 2 (2015 - 16)

During this year, we had the opportunity to add an additional course to our individually tailored schedules. Gustav Svensson and I decided to choose Massage. We discussed it together, and I chose it as a tribute to my dear uncle, Farbror Hasse, who was an educated masseuse. He used to give me massages whenever we met, and I wanted to honour his influence in my life by learning the skills he had mastered.

In addition to the Massage course, I also chose to study Danish. I've always been fascinated by our neighbouring country, particularly because of their liberal views on drugs and their unique free-town called Malmö. Danish culture intrigued me, and I saw this as an opportunity to learn more about it firsthand.

These two classes, Massage and Danish, were added to my schedule in 2016. They represented not only my interests but also a connection to important influences in my life—my uncle and my fascination with Denmark.

Despite my lingering vices—spending countless hours on computers, indulging in video games, and fueling my entrepreneurial spirit through selling drugs—I never missed a single Tuesday or Thursday when the massage course had its lectures. There was something about that class that captivated me. Maybe it was the calming atmosphere that stood in stark contrast to the chaos of my other pursuits, or perhaps it was the hands-on nature of learning that grounded me in a way that traditional schooling never could. Those sessions were more than just classes; they were a break from the relentless pace of my life, a rare moment where I could focus on something that felt almost therapeutic. In a world where I constantly pushed the boundaries, that massage course became an unexpected anchor, offering a brief escape from my otherwise turbulent days.

On a day that started like so many others, when skipping school was just another part of my routine, I found myself making my usual trip to Malmö. My mission was clear: pick up a kilo of hashish. As I approached the familiar spot in Lorensborg, there was a strange comfort in the predictability of it all—until that comfort shattered in an instant.

Leffe, standing with his usual calm demeanor, met my eyes and asked, "Hey Hugo, do you know anyone who wants to buy 20 hand grenades for 10,000?"

The question slammed into me like a sudden chill, making my breath catch. I blurted out before I could think, "Are you fucking serious?"

Leffe's expression didn't change. His eyes were as cold and steady as ever, his voice flat and unwavering. "Yes," he said, without missing a beat. "Do you know someone?"

The air around us seemed to thicken. I could hear the distant sound of traffic, a dog barking somewhere nearby, the ordinary noises of the city suddenly muted by the weight of his question. For a moment, time slowed as I processed what he had just asked. This wasn't just a simple transaction anymore; this was something much darker, more dangerous. The stakes had changed, and with them, so had the game.

Yet, instead of pushing me away, the gravity of the situation pulled me in. There was an unexpected exhilaration, a pulse of adrenaline that surged through my veins. I looked at Leffe, this man who spoke of weapons with the same detachment as he might a grocery list, and I felt a strange sense of awe. His calm authority, the way he seemed untouchable in a world where danger was currency, made him appear larger than life.

It was in that moment that I realized I was already too deep, the line between hustling and something far more perilous blurred beyond recognition. And I was stepping over it willingly, driven not just by profit, but by the rush of being part of something bigger, something that was teetering dangerously close to the edge.

Gloria and I would often have deep conversations, confiding in each other about our hopes, dreams, and worries. Whether we were sitting in her room, surrounded by posters and the soft hum of our favorite music playing in the background, or taking leisurely walks through the neighborhood as the sun dipped behind the houses, there was an unspoken understanding between us. We'd share stories that reached deep into our pasts and dreams that stretched far into the future, exploring who we wanted to become and what we were afraid might hold us back.

Sometimes, a shared laugh would break the tension of serious topics, leaving us with the warm comfort of knowing that, no matter how heavy the world felt, we weren't facing it alone. I sometimes wonder if those talks were as grounding for her as they were for me, giving us both a space where we could be fully honest and vulnerable without judgment. In those moments, the bond between us felt unbreakable—a quiet, reassuring connection that added light even on the cloudiest days.

There was this one time when I went to pick up a kilo from Santiago, Leffe's acquaintance—a transaction I assumed would go as smoothly as the others. But Santiago, as I would learn, was full of surprises.

The brick he handed me was far from the usual 100-gram slabs of high-quality hashish I was accustomed to. This one was wrapped tightly in golden foil, with Arabic symbols etched around the words *"Lucky 27."* It looked impressive, almost ceremonial, like something that had travelled far to reach Malmö.

But appearances can be deceiving. When I tried it, I immediately knew it was trash—pure henna. It had a texture that crumbled too easily, and the smell was off, lacking the rich, earthy aroma of proper hash. I gave Santiago a skeptical look.

"This is what you're selling me?" I asked, holding up the brick.

"It's golden stamp," he said, his tone defensive. "Top quality. You'll see."

Charles Ingvar, who was hanging out with me at the time, took a lighter and burned a gram right there, treating it like a candle more than something worth smoking. The way it fizzled and burned confirmed what I already knew: this was garbage.

"I'm not paying for this," I said, setting the brick down on the table.

But Santiago wasn't one to back down easily. He leaned forward, his eyes narrowing. "You've already taken it. You're paying for it."

I refused to budge, but the tension in the room grew thick. Santiago's insistence was as relentless as his shady dealings, and I realized then that he wasn't just a lousy supplier—he was someone who didn't take no for an answer.

I ended up leaving with the brick, not because I wanted it but because Santiago made it clear I didn't have much of a choice. That incident stuck with me, not just because of the terrible product but because it showed me the lengths he'd go to protect his reputation and get his way. It was one of many red flags I should have paid more attention to.

School Year 3 (2016 - 17)

During this period, my cannabis operation had grown into what could be considered a "full-scale" business, moving multiple kilos a month—an impressive scale, especially given the ages of those involved. I had four primary connections for sourcing the narcotics:

- Dejanovic
- Leffe
- Calle
- M.H.

Occasionally, I also reached out to other contacts for smaller pickups.

Cannabis wasn't the only substance in my inventory; amphetamine, ecstasy, MDMA, and LSD were also part of the trade. At my peak, I was earning between 25,000 to 30,000 SEK per month, all while consuming more than 5 grams of hashish daily.

Despite our best efforts to operate under the radar, our activities hadn't gone unnoticed. The media had reported on drug sales in Ystad a few times[1], which drew some unwanted attention. But what concerned me more was that larger criminal organizations had begun to take note of my growing presence.

This event started out as usual - someone refers a client to me, in this context it was a friend from Kunskapsskolan called K-O who asked if I could sell 50g of skunk to his god-father. I say, yes, of course. I start communicating

---

[1] www.ystadsallehanda.se/ystad/ystad-ar-som-christiania/

with K-O's godfather on the application that we regularly used for the sale of drugs—"Wickr".

A couple of hours later I leave Gloria in the bedroom, I don't remember exactly what she was doing at that point in time but looking back I can imagine that she was playing Sims as she usually did. At that time I lived in the apartment right across from Subway on the shopping street of Ystad—the street address was Stora Östergatan 8. I kissed Gloria on the forehead and told her that I will be right back.

When I leave the apartment I go to the designated drop off point by the parking of the church along the square—I notice 3 people standing and waiting by a car whilst I circle around the square with a plastic grocery bag with a jam-jar filled with skunk and a scale. It was late at night and no one else was out. I feel a bit uneasy for some reason, but, seeing as K-O referred the client, I approached the car with the three individuals standing beside it.

I immediately greet them and sit down in the front passenger seat with my "Coop Konsum" bag confirming if it's 50 grams of skunk that they want. The godfather told me that I was sitting in the wrong place and asked me if I could sit in the backseat instead. I felt ridiculous taking liberties sitting in the front in a strangers car—so I changed seats to sit in the back.

There I sit next to the bearded godfather and scale up 50 grams of cannabis in front of him and conduct the sale for 3500 crowns. 70 crowns a gram, netting only 500 crowns in the transaction—friendly favour to K-O letting go of the luxurious skunk for that small of a price. The godfather told me that I shouldn't tell anyone at the club about what occurred and I realised that this godfather figure is actually a career criminal involved in organised crime and by "club" he refers to the crime syndicate he was a part of.

When I came back to Gloria, I was a bit stirred up and let her know that I met a heavy criminal person involved in organised crime—a person that exists on Google and such and I was a bit baffled. She was barely surprised if I remember correctly.

Ironically enough, around this time, I got in contact with a Mexican drug cartel known as the Sinaloa Cartel and proposed a business deal. I promised that I could put together an operation that would yield them 100,000 SEK in profit every single month solely on cannabis. My plan was to introduce them to the different dealers I knew, thus enabling them to become the primary supplier to multiple criminal networks in the underground of Malmö.

The idea seemed brilliant in its simplicity. By leveraging my extensive network of contacts within Malmö's criminal underworld, I believed I could create a streamlined and efficient supply chain that would not only meet the high demand for drugs but also ensure a steady flow of profits. I envisioned myself as the linchpin, the crucial connector between the Sinaloa Cartel and the local dealers who needed a reliable and potent source of product.

The initial conversations were tense and filled with a mix of excitement and fear. The stakes were incredibly high, and the potential consequences of failure were severe. However, I was driven by the promise of success and the thrill of orchestrating such a significant operation. I meticulously mapped out my strategy, identifying key players and potential challenges, and prepared to dive into the world of high-stakes drug trafficking.

As I moved forward with the plan, the reality of dealing with a powerful and ruthless cartel began to set in. Every interaction carried an undercurrent of danger, and the pressure to deliver on my promises was immense. Despite the risks, I remained focused on my goal, determined to prove that I could handle the demands of this dangerous game. The path I had chosen was fraught with peril, but the potential rewards were too great to ignore.

They were very trusting and reliable. At that time, I had over 80,000 SEK in credit extended to various people, and I was forced to take a loan myself to pay back two dealers to whom I was indebted. This was the curse of being a dealer who was not only crediting out substances but also consuming large volumes of narcotics himself. The constant balancing act between managing debts and maintaining supply was a relentless and stressful cycle.

I borrowed 32,600 SEK from Double D, whom Adam Palm (may his soul rest in peace) had introduced me to, and 20,000 SEK from the Sinaloa Cartel in order to pay back Leffe and Dejanovic. The pressure of owing money to such dangerous figures was immense. Double D was known for his ruthless business practices, and the Sinaloa Cartel was infamous for its unforgiving approach to debts.

My days were a whirlwind of drug deals, calculations, and anxiety. The loans temporarily alleviated the immediate financial burden, but they also added a new layer of risk and responsibility. The stakes were higher than ever, and any misstep could have catastrophic consequences. Despite the constant tension, I managed to maintain a facade of control and confidence, navigating this treacherous world with a mixture of determination and desperation.

As I worked to repay these significant loans, I also had to continue my operations, ensuring that my network remained intact and that my clients stayed satisfied. The balancing act was precarious, and the stress took its toll, but I was driven by the need to survive and succeed in this high-stakes environment.

The deal I made with Double D, a larger gangster covered in tattoos, with huge muscles and American bullies, was to borrow 32,600 SEK. When I arrived at his apartment, I was greeted by an intimidating sight: a gun laying on the table and an American bully roaming freely.

Despite the intimidating environment, I knew I had to prove my worth. I pulled out my computer and brought up Excel documents, showing him detailed records of my transactions and assets. I demonstrated that I had significant value to my name and was worthy of credit.

Double D scrutinised the documents, his expression unreadable. The atmosphere was tense as I awaited his verdict, the weight of the gun on the table serving as a stark reminder of the potential consequences of failure. Finally, after what felt like an eternity, he nodded in approval, acknowledging my credibility.

He opened up a drawer and pulled out a stack of cash and started counting it up on the living room table. 32,000. Exactly what I needed.

The loan was a lifeline, allowing me to pay back my debts to Leffe and Dejanovic and keep my operation afloat. However, it also came with strings attached, binding me further into the dangerous world of high-stakes drug dealing. The encounter with Double D amongst the other criminal figures that I met was a stark reminder of the perilous path I had chosen, where every decision carried significant risks and the margin for error was nonexistent.

Despite the constant pressure and danger, I remained determined to navigate this treacherous landscape. The experience reinforced my resolve to stay one step ahead, using every ounce of my resourcefulness and resilience to survive and succeed.

I did, however, take a personal liking to Double D. Despite his intimidating exterior, he was a philosophical fellow with an interest in listening to the lectures of Alan Watts, a teacher I greatly admired and spent a lot of time listening to.

"A man ceases to exist without his vices," is a quote that I have lived by. My guilty pleasure has always been lying in a hammock, my mind enchanted by LSD, and listening to Watts' lectures for hours at a time.

Double D's shared interest in Alan Watts created an unexpected bond between us. We would occasionally discuss the profound ideas and philosophies presented in

Watts' teachings, finding common ground despite the vastly different paths our lives had taken. This connection added a layer of complexity to our relationship, making it more than just a transactional arrangement.

Through our conversations, I began to see a different side of Double D, one that was contemplative and introspective. It was a stark contrast to the hardened exterior he presented to the world. This duality fascinated me and deepened my desire to befriend him. I hoped that our shared philosophical interests could lead to a meaningful friendship, even in the midst of the dangerous and chaotic world we both inhabited.

In the end, this bond was both a comfort and a reminder of the multifaceted nature of the people involved in the underground world. It showed me that even in the darkest places, there can be moments of genuine connection and understanding.

Strangely enough, I didn't speak to a single soul about the business deal I made with the Sinaloa Cartel. I felt no need whatsoever to let others know about my plans. This secrecy was crucial for maintaining control and ensuring the operation ran smoothly without unnecessary complications.

Keeping such a significant aspect of my life hidden required a considerable amount of discipline and caution.

I knew that any leak or loose talk could jeopardise not only the deal but also my safety and the safety of those around me. The stakes were incredibly high, and I couldn't afford to let anyone get wind of my involvement with such a powerful and dangerous organisation.

Despite the isolation this secrecy brought, it also provided me with a sense of autonomy and power. I was the sole architect of this plan, responsible for every detail and decision. The burden of this responsibility was heavy, but it also fuelled my determination to succeed.

I still remember my first physical meeting with the Sinaloa Cartel. I was bold enough to ask if my handler could pick up Gloria and me from a location in Malmö after we had been out on some trivial activity, like spending time with friends or going on a date. These were activities I always felt were important but could possibly wait until I had "beaten the game" of my criminal endeavours. I always felt like I was close to achieving something big.

Gloria was told that a taxi was coming to pick us up, supposedly to drop her off at the station and then drive me to a friend's place. We got into the backseat of the car without exchanging a single word with the driver, aside from a formal greeting. When we arrived at "Triangeln," one of the two central stations in Malmö, I jumped out of the car with Gloria, kissed her goodbye, told her I loved her, and informed her that I would be coming home late.

Although we never had our own place, we sort of lived together, spending some days at her parents' place and some at mine. One thing was certain: we were always together, no matter what, except when I was consuming narcotics (aside from cannabis) or conducting business transactions. As a rule of thumb, at least. There were always exceptions.

After saying goodbye to Gloria, I got back into the car, this time in the front seat. We drove off, and I began pitching my ideas. I explained how I could establish a powerful operation for them within two to three weeks, ensuring a monthly figure akin to a pension. We arrived at a restaurant, whose name shall remain unmentioned to protect the cartel operative's identity, as security footage could be used for identification.

Our conversation carried on over dinner, the tension gradually easing as we found common ground. The man's sharp gaze softened with interest and understanding, his posture exuding calm authority. As we shared ideas and discussed logistics, I felt a strange mix of fear and exhilaration—fear of what I was stepping into and exhilaration at the possibilities this connection could bring.

On the ride back to the station, the gravity of the moment settled in. I wanted to show my seriousness, to demonstrate that I wasn't just another small-time player. So, out of a mix of trust and calculated risk, I handed over my passport—a token of commitment to the operation.

On top of the passport, I included a ledger, meticulously prepared with the names and contact details of key players I planned to introduce them to in the future. These were individuals who had established themselves in Malmö's underground scene, and their involvement could provide the cartel with a strong foothold in the region.

In return, they handed me a stack of crisp 500-kronor bills, meticulously bundled with a paper tag labeled "20,000." It was a professional exchange, marked by precision and mutual understanding. These were seasoned players, and their efficiency was both impressive and intimidating.

As I held the money in my hands, I realized the weight of my choices. This wasn't just a transaction—it was a step deeper into a world where loyalty and ruthlessness went hand in hand.

I also followed him on an errand in order to pick up 68k SEK in cash from one of his employees, he counted it in the driver seat sitting next to me.

This meeting marked the beginning of a significant chapter in my life, where the stakes were high, and the risks were even higher. Despite the gravity of the situation, I felt a strange sense of exhilaration, as if I was on the brink of something monumental.

You can probably imagine why I found it trivial and, to be honest, difficult to be present in school consistently enough to perform well. While I didn't have any issues understanding the material or performing when I was actually in class, maintaining regular attendance was a significant challenge for me. This inconsistency inevitably affected my grades, despite my capabilities.

I continued selling narcotics to people in my town and even extended my network to players from other cities in Skåne, operating under the Wickr handle "UltranSkane." As my business grew, so did the challenges, especially when it came to collecting debts. It reached a point where I realised I needed some help. The next time I met up with K-O's Godfather, I asked if he could assist me in collecting some of the outstanding debts.

Here's a list of what was owed:

M	QT	4000	50b	Sep. 2016
M	A.W	3000	50b	Sep. 2016

M	P.E	3000	50b	Sep. 2016
M	I.B	6000	100b	
M		5100	100B, 500 lån	
Mudda		5000		
KemiMagi		7000		

These weren't huge amounts individually, but collectively, they added up to what I needed to repay the Sinaloa Cartel. The total came to 21,000 SEK, and after deducting the Godfather's collection fee of 5,000 SEK, I was left with 16,000 SEK. That month, I managed to pull in over 30,000 SEK in net profits, mostly from MDMA sales that I had on credit from Dejanovic, while also collecting some debts myself. I was close to paying off the loan from Double D when he suddenly raised the amount I owed to 50,000 SEK from the original 32,000 SEK.

Feeling betrayed, I decided to consult with the Godfather during one of those long nights where I'd been up for almost two days straight, fuelled by amphetamines and benzodiazepines. The Godfather asked me bluntly: "Do you want to have any relationship whatsoever with Double D after this?"

And I regretfully reply: "No."

If I remember correctly, I had already paid him back 29,000 SEK. That night, with the Godfather in his MC vest, we gathered our crew, determined to confront Double D about his extortion tactics. We needed to sort out the deal for the original 32,000 SEK as initially agreed upon. We drove to his place under the cover of darkness. When he came down to open the door, we were ready. One soldier stood 10 meters behind me and the Godfather, another was positioned 10 meters to the left, all strategically placed to make sure Double D knew this wasn't just a casual visit.

When Double D opened the door, his face paled as he saw me standing there with three men, all wearing motorcycle vests. The Godfather wasted no time and got straight to the point.

"You borrowed Hugo 32 grand, and that's exactly what you're getting back. Here's the remaining 3,000," he said, handing over the cash.

Double D stammered "But... I was only trying to show him what other, less kind people might do..." Before he could finish, the Godfather cut him off, his voice cold and menacing.

"If you don't shut the fuck up right now, I'm putting a knife in your throat. Nod if you understand." Double D's eyes widened with fear, and he nodded quickly.

"Now, shake hands with Hugo and say that your deal is done. You two won't have anything to do with each other anymore," the Godfather ordered.

I reached out, and Double D reluctantly shook my hand, mumbling something about the deal being over. The tension in the air was thick, but the message was clear: our business was finished.

That night, the Godfather made sure every one of the vested men who had helped was paid for their part in the operation. Once everything was settled, I finally crashed at Gloria's place, completely drained after being awake for more than two days straight. Sleep came quickly, a welcome escape from the chaos of the past few days.

But it didn't last long. I was jolted awake by Gloria shaking me. Two guys from the M-phalanx had been bombarding Gloria with messages on Facebook. My heart raced as I wondered if they were Double D's friends seeking revenge.

I called the Godfather immediately to let him know what was happening. Without missing a beat, he assured me, "I'll send cars to sit outside the apartment to protect you."

I hesitated, "But, I don't think that's necessary."

His response was firm, "I am in command. We don't take any risks."

With that, I knew I was safe, at least for the time being. The Godfather's word was law, and when he said there would be no risks, he meant it.

We eventually managed to talk things out with the M-Phalanx, and no further action was necessary. The tension eased, and I was finally able to return to a deep, undisturbed sleep, momentarily forgetting all the chaos. But as I lay there, I couldn't shake the realisation of what I was putting Gloria through. The danger I brought into her life weighed heavily on my conscience.

In the days that followed, I made the difficult decision to break things off with her. It was one of the hardest choices I've ever made, but I knew I couldn't continue to involve her in my criminal world. The risks were too great, and I couldn't bear the thought of something happening to her because of me. The regret hit hard, but I knew it was the right thing to do.

After the breakup, I decided it was time to leave my mother's place as well. I moved into one of my client's (Lurifilur) apartments, renting a room in his small two-room flat. At first, I had nothing but a mattress on the floor, but slowly and steadily, I started to build a new space for myself. It wasn't much, but it was mine, and for the first time in a while, I felt like I was beginning to carve out a place for myself, away from the dangers and the shadows of my past.

During this time, I was nudged into the decision to drop out of school by my brother, Calle. His reasoning was clear: there wasn't much point in being enrolled when I had neither the possibility nor the will to attend. Despite this, I chose to stay enrolled, even though I rarely, if ever, showed up. When summer 2017 rolled around and my classmates were celebrating their graduation, I received my report card. It was a stark reminder of the road I had chosen—or perhaps the road I had been pushed down:

1. **English 5** (ENGENG05) - **C**
2. **English 6** (ENGENG06) - **D**
3. **English 7** (ENGENG07) - **F**
4. **Philosophy 1** (FIOFI001) - **F**
5. **History 1b** (HISHIS01b) - **F**
6. **Humanistic and Social Science Specialization** (HUMHUMOOS) - **F**
7. **Physical Education and Health 1** (IDRIDR01) - ---
8. **Communication** (PEDKOUO) - **F**
9. **Massage 1** - **E**
10. **Leadership and Organization** (LEDLEDO) - **F**
11. **Mathematics 1b** (MATMAT01b) - **F**

12. **Mathematics 2b** (MATMAT02b) - **F**
13. **Mental Training** (HALMENO) - **F**
14. **Modern Languages 1** (MODDAN01) - --- (Danish)
15. **Modern Languages 2** (MODDAN02) - **F** (Danish)
16. **Natural Science 1b** (NAKNAK01b) - **F**
17. **Psychology 1** (PSKPSY01) - **F**
18. **Psychology 2a** (PSKPSY02a) - **F**
19. **Religious Studies 1** (RELREL01) - **F**
20. **Law and Society** (JURRÄTO) - **F**
21. **Social Studies 1b** (SAMSAM01b) - **F**
22. **Social Studies 2** (SAMSAM02) - **F**
23. **Sociology** (SOISOOO) - **F**
24. **Swedish 1** (SVESVE01) - **F**
25. **Swedish 2** (SVESVE02) - **F**
26. **Swedish 3** (SVESVE03) - **F**
27. **High School Project SA** (GYARSA) - **F**
28. **Criminology** - **F**

These grades were the result of 93% absenteeism over my three years in high school. The numbers don't lie, and they painted a bleak picture of a path not taken, of opportunities missed, of potential wasted.

Looking back, it's easy to wonder: what if? What if I had made the decision to follow in the footsteps of Charles Ingvar and paid some of my classmates to complete my assignments? Or, what if I had simply attended class, put in the effort, and tried to engage, even just a little?

It's a tough pill to swallow, realising that the decisions I made back then have cast such long shadows over my life. But hindsight, as they say, is 20/20. The lessons learned from those years, though hard-earned, are invaluable. They serve as a constant reminder of the importance of showing up—for school, for life, for myself. And though I can't change the past, I can use it to shape a better future.

Calle moved into Lurifilur's place after a while, and it soon turned into a junkie-paradise or traphouse, with us inhabitants continuously consuming narcotics and smoking cannabis without doing anything else. I remember waking up one morning in my room, then wandering to the other rooms where Lurifilur usually slept on the couch. There, I saw both my brother and Luri, passed out, half on the couch and half on the floor. I took a photo and kept it as a memory on my Snapchat account.

Reflecting on it now, I realise I was only supposed to stay at Lurifilur's place temporarily until I could work things out with Gloria. At least, that's what I recall from a text conversation we had. Perhaps that was my way of convincing myself and Lurifilur that it was just a temporary arrangement. I told myself, "I just need to crash here until I have worked everything out with Gloria," but in reality, I ended up turning his apartment into a drug den.

Writing all of this down is triggering so many memories. I was high as hell on benzodiazepines when I broke up with Gloria—or so I thought. Now, as I truly reflect, I'm not so sure if I was the one who initiated the breakup. Gloria came to visit me at Lurifilur's place, where I was sleeping on a mattress on the floor, high, doped up, and traumatised. And then she left me.

Perhaps, in my drugged and confused state, I've been telling myself that I broke up with her because I didn't want to involve her in my criminal activities, thinking that was what made sense. But maybe, just maybe, I was the one left behind, unable to remember or accept the truth. This realisation hits me hard, challenging the narrative I've held onto.

Will I ever find out what truly happened in that drug-haze where I lost the love of my life, our family dog, moved out from my mother's apartment and lost 80 grand? I don't think so.

There came a time, after I had moved out from Lurifilur's place, when I found myself in a tough spot. I ended up staying over at my childhood friend Amanda Sjöstedt's place, practically homeless. I was too proud to move back into my mother's home. The thought of returning there felt like admitting defeat, like running back with my tail between my legs. I couldn't face that kind of failure, so I chose to wander through those uncertain days, crashing wherever I could, rather than go back to where I started. It was a tough period, but my pride and determination kept me going, pushing me to find another way forward.

Notes: but before that I tripped balls on over 900 UG liquid cristal needle grateful dead LSD in the forest and have visuals, I suppose, of being surrounded by the government field group (socialtjänsten) and military.

I had just gone through a series of terrible events[2]— physically and mentally abused, I found myself trapped in the claws of a criminal network. It was a dark time, and unfortunately, I didn't seek help until it was nearly too late. My ambitions, relationships, and hope slowly withered away, leaving me in a state of desperation. I found myself at Amanda's place, numbing the pain by popping pills. It was there that Ronja Moreno[3], who was consuming the same pills with me, had a severe epilepsy

---

[2] With physical and mental abuse "forcing" me into a drug addiction, the loss of 80 000 SEK and giving up our family dog, Bobby.

[3] Ronja later on changed her name to Sacha.

attack and almost died. The report later revealed that the pills were laced with fentanyl, a fact I could hardly believe, considering how much I trusted the source.

Mami was living with her child, her boyfriend, Anton. When Ronja's attack happened, Anton, knowing I was carrying narcotics, told me to leave immediately while he arranged for an ambulance. Following his instructions, I left, with nowhere to go but the train station. With no other options and a heavy heart, I departed for Denmark—the place where I had always planned to start my next chapter. I had studied Danish in school and had always been curious about the liberal country just across the water.

I choose not to delve into the specifics of those dark incidents. I don't want to point fingers, and frankly, I fear that digging into those old memories might turn them into potholes filled with enemies. What's in the past should stay there. There's no need to bring it forward; some things are better left buried in the shadows of yesterday.

Denmark (2017 - 2019)

I remember the moment I arrived in Copenhagen as if it were etched into my soul. With nothing but a meagre handful of crumpled bills and a heavy heart, I stumbled off the train, the weight of my failures bearing down on me like an anchor dragging me to the depths. The city, so vibrant and alive, seemed indifferent to my plight. In a haze of disillusionment, I made my way to a small, unremarkable shop and bought a bottle of vodka—a pitiful, temporary escape from the crushing reality of my existence.

I found solace—or perhaps only the illusion of it—in a worn-out lounge set by Istegade, a place that seemed as broken and defeated as I felt. The velvet cushions were stained and the wood scratched, but it was here that I chose to sit, drowning my sorrows in a bitter sea of vodka. As the cold, sharp liquid burned its way down my throat, I stared out at the world around me, feeling the weight of my regrets and the overwhelming sense of failure. The streets, bustling with life and laughter, were a stark contrast to the desolation I felt within.

I had lost everything that once mattered to me—my dreams, my hopes, and the illusions of a future I had imagined. Now, all that remained was a hollow shell of a man, grappling with the haunting realisation that my life had unravelled into a series of missteps and missed opportunities. The vodka, while numbing, could not drown out the relentless echo of my mistakes, and the city continued to spin around me, indifferent to the shattered pieces of my existence.

Eventually, as if summoned by some celestial intervention, a glimmer of hope pierced through the veil of my despair. The universe, in its mysterious ways, decided to cast a spotlight on my beleaguered soul. It happened when two strikingly beautiful Norwegian women, radiant and full of life, took a seat next to me. Their names were Amalie and Emelie.

Amalie had a presence that seemed to brighten the very air around her. Her laughter, a melodic chime, cut through my melancholy like a beacon of warmth. Emelie, with her eyes that sparkled like the fjords of her homeland, brought with her an air of effortless grace. As they settled into the lounge, their conversation began to weave its way into my solitude, filling the space with a sense of connection that I hadn't felt in what seemed like an eternity.

Their presence was transformative. The contrast between their vivacity and my despondency was stark, yet somehow, it was this very contrast that began to lift the fog of my misery. They spoke with a sincerity and kindness that gradually softened the edges of my sorrow. As we exchanged stories and laughter, the weight of my regrets seemed to momentarily lift, replaced by the lightness of human connection and the promise of new beginnings. It was as if these two strangers, with their own stories and experiences, were sent to remind me of the beauty that could still be found in the most unexpected places.

It didn't take long for the scene to shift from a quiet respite to a lively gathering. The lounge where I had sought solace suddenly became a nexus of social energy as two young men, both around twenty-five, joined us. They brought with them a palpable sense of enthusiasm and an eagerness to engage, adding a new dimension to the evening's unfolding drama.

With their arrival, the night took on a more vibrant tone. The conversation flowed with increasing ease, and as the hours wore on, the group's collective thirst for merriment led to more rounds of alcohol—this time generously funded by our new acquaintances, as my own finances had been exhausted. Their generosity opened up new possibilities, and soon we found ourselves heading to their place, a stylish apartment that promised a change of pace.

The evening continued to spiral into a whirlwind of unexpected pleasures. In the intimacy of their chic surroundings, I found myself sharing a night of intense connection with Amalie. Our time together was a stark contrast to the solitude I had felt earlier, a passionate and engaging encounter that temporarily dissolved the weight of my previous despair. As the night stretched on, the alcohol and the heat of the moment led to an impromptu sleepover in their upscale abode.

Amid the afterglow of the evening, one of the hosts, curious about the capsules I had brought along, asked if they were cocaine and whether he could buy some. His question was met with a dry laugh from me. I explained that the capsules were pregabalin—my own form of "happy pills"—a necessity for keeping my mind alert and grounded. It was a small, perhaps incongruous detail, but in the midst of the night's revelry, it seemed to fit right in with the oddity of the situation.

I ended up crashing on the couch that night, and in the morning, I was gently woken by this lovely man who took me to the local store. We picked up some fresh groceries, went back to his place, and cooked a meal together. Later, we decided to go for a swim, embracing the heat of the summer day.

While we were at the bridge, in a spontaneous burst of energy, I attempted—and miraculously succeeded at—a backflip for the first (and only) time in my life. The thrill of that moment was pure and unfiltered.

I had an incredible time with him, though, sadly, his name escapes me now. After spending that time together, I found myself wandering along Istedgade, seeking a way to numb the anxiety that had plagued me since the breakup with Gloria. It led me to a dark decision: scoring some heroin.

For the first time in my life, I smoked heroin. The sensation was so overwhelmingly euphoric that I couldn't help but cry tears of joy. It was an intoxicating mix of relief and release, a brief escape from the turmoil that had been swirling in my mind. But even in that moment of bliss, there was an underlying awareness of the dangerous path I was treading.

I had lost everything—my ties to friends and family, a once-splendid relationship, and any semblance of stability. What was left for me to lose? The weight of my losses pressed down on me, and I couldn't help but wonder what had happened to the deal I was in the middle of with the Sinaloa Cartel. It seemed like everything I had worked for, including the vision of a secure future for me and Gloria, had crumbled into dust. The dream of a life without financial regrets, where we could establish a future together, felt like a distant, unattainable fantasy.

With nowhere else to turn, I drifted around Istegade, that infamous street in Copenhagen, where the remnants of broken lives gathered. I found myself frequenting H17, a place that seemed to embody my descent into darkness. H17 is one of those government-sanctioned buildings where people can go inside, register, and then enter specific rooms designed for the usage of narcotics. They have both injection rooms and smoking rooms, spaces where the walls have absorbed the desperation and fleeting relief of countless others.

I smoked crack cocaine and heroin there, losing myself in the haze of addiction. The irony of it all struck me— here I was, in a place where the government provided the tools to slowly destroy myself, yet it was the only place where I felt a semblance of belonging. The once-clear path I had envisioned for myself was now shrouded in a fog of despair, with each hit pulling me further away from the future I had once so desperately wanted.

At some point, I found myself sleeping on a mattress on the floor at Mændenes Hjem, a shelter in Istegade. When I woke up, I realised that both my bag and my watch had been stolen while I slept. The watch was an Inex, purchased in 1999 for 1250 crowns by my uncle,

Hasse. It wasn't just a watch; it was a deeply sentimental piece, a connection to someone I cared about.

My bag held many things, but the most important was a business card given to me by Atilla, with the contact of a government official in Hungary who could have helped me establish a base there. The loss of the watch, combined with the loss of that crucial contact, left me feeling utterly defeated.

In a moment of desperation, I reached out to Double D's, telling him that losing everything, including my uncle's watch, was enough to push me over the edge—enough to make me consider becoming a full-time crack addict without any remorse for life. His response cut through my despair. He simply asked, "Is that really what your uncle would have wanted for you?"

In those moments, sitting in the smoky confines of H17, I realised just how much I had lost. Not just the tangible things—relationships, deals, dreams—but also a part of myself that I feared I would never recover. The abyss I had fallen into seemed endless, with no clear way out. Yet, amid the numbing effects of the drugs, a tiny, persistent thought lingered: How did it come to this? And could I ever find my way back?

After some time, I began touring around town, starting to see this period as something surreal—a twisted kind of vacation. Yes, a vacation as a homeless vagabond, sleeping on the streets and in various homeless shelters. It was a strange way to view my circumstances, but in the chaos of it all, it felt like the only way to cope.

I often found myself in Malmö, a place that became a sanctuary of sorts. It was a colourful, vibrant area, known for its free-spirited community and open-air drug market. There, I could relax, enjoy the atmosphere, and be treated to joints by people who were just as lost in their own worlds as I was. Malmö was a melting pot of individuals from all walks of life—artists, drifters, dreamers. It was a place where no one asked too many questions, and everyone was welcome, regardless of their past or present.

During one of my visits, I met an older poet, a kind soul who took me under his wing. He saw something in my scribbled notes and encouraged me to turn them into something more. Together, we worked on my first rap song, a raw reflection of my life and struggles. The song was like a mirror, reflecting the chaos, the highs and lows, and the relentless search for meaning in a world that seemed to have lost all sense.

I can't remember the entire song—there were 12 verses, I think—but some parts still echo in my mind:

Verse 1: Yo, I remember back in the days
When I was psychotic, melancholic
Nading people's houses, getting chased by the mob
Hooking pieces for the jobs, flipping my wishes
To feed some vices, smoking some ice, and
Levitating just nice

Verse 2: I have trouble living in the present
I keep on living in my own bubble
Where I am the only resident
The President

Verse 3: I used to rely on what
I knew was false hope
Just so I could blow
Myself through some dope

Verse 4: I became waxy, too lucid
The different planes
Keep merging in my mind
And yet I feel so stupid

Chorus: Hope for the better
Crazy how life goes
Reality blows the illusion
Confusion, lost lives
Deranged, running in a trap
Performing a hectic rap

The poet helped me shape these thoughts into something tangible, something that captured the essence of my journey. The process of writing and rapping those verses felt like an exorcism of sorts—getting the demons out of my head and onto paper, where I could see them for what they were. Even though the song was unfinished, it became a piece of my story, a reminder of a time when I was drifting but still fighting to hold on to something real.

His name was Ole Flindt, I won't ever forget his name. He allowed me to visit his place and take care of my needs such as showering and cutting my toenails there. He was a good man.

One day, I was walking the streets, minding my own business on the way towards Malmö, when I noticed a tall man with long hair and a mighty beard unpacking his trailer loaded with crepe wagons. Curiosity piqued, I approached him and asked, "Sir, do you need some help unpacking the wagon?"

To my surprise, he replied, "No, but I need some dependable workers."

And just like that, I got my job as a crepes salesman. It was a lesson in the importance of communication and networking; being polite never hurts and can sometimes lead to unexpected opportunities.

During that time, I slept at a homeless shelter located at Hillerødgade 138—an address I still remember vividly, haha! I would wake up at 6 every morning to go to work selling crepes. That period of my life was surprisingly enjoyable—who could have imagined that selling crepes could be so fun?

Now, as I reflect on those days, I wonder if my opportunity to import the JuraMajs Crepes Wagons franchise into Sweden has been lost or if it's still a possibility. The idea of bringing those delightful crepes to a new market still excites me, and I hope to make it a reality someday.

One evening, after a long day of wandering, I arrived at the shelter hoping for a good night's sleep. I brought along some dirty clothes that desperately needed washing. As I woke up the next morning, I noticed a staff member I hadn't seen before. Wanting to get my laundry done, I approached him and asked if he could help me out.

With a kind smile, he said, "Why yes, of course. I can help you wash your clothes." Together, we loaded the laundry machine, and I decided to stick around the shelter while my clothes were being cleaned. We struck up a conversation, and I quickly learned that this helpful man was called Mission. He was the caretaker of the place, and since I didn't have work that day, I ended up spending most of the day at the shelter, chatting with him.

As lunchtime rolled around, Mission invited me to join him in the cafeteria at Hillerödgade. He insisted on treating me, and we shared a simple meal together. Looking back, I realise that it might have been against the rules for him to interact with a client in such a personal way, but Mission did it anyway, and through our conversations, we began to get to know each other on a deeper level.

Later that day, I headed over to Malmö to clear my mind and score some smoke. I found myself sitting down at a café called Woodstock, playing backgammon with strangers. As the game unfolded, my thoughts drifted back to everything I had been through—the violence I had suffered, the painful breakup with Gloria, my hasty escape from Sweden, and the life I had left behind.

Santiago's name had already carried weight long before it reached me. It wasn't just whispered—it lingered, soaked in the murky infamy of Pusher Street. Conversations in dimly lit corners often included his name, usually in hushed tones, as if merely saying it too loud might summon trouble. His reputation wasn't one of direct confrontation or raw violence, but something darker, more insidious.

"He's the kind who works in shadows," Leffe had once said, his tone cold. "The kind of scum you don't notice until it's too late." I stopped working as a Crepes salesman and did instead choose to go the route underground.

In that moment of reflection, I felt a pull to reconnect with the cartel. I reached out to them, and to my surprise, they responded with unexpected generosity. They gave me the key and address to an apartment in Denmark, telling me, "Help yourself out."

Their offer caught me off guard, but I understood their motives. I was an associate who had fallen on hard times, and they saw value in helping me out. It wasn't just about charity; it was about maintaining ties, ensuring that I remained useful to them in the future. And so, with a mix of gratitude and caution, I accepted their offer, knowing that it would bring me closer to the life I had once tried to escape, but also recognising that it was my best chance at survival.

I spent the next few hours cleaning up the place, moving furniture around and trying to make the apartment liveable again. It was clear that the space had been abandoned for quite some time, judging by the thick layers of dust covering everything. The furniture was piled up haphazardly, almost as if the apartment had been used as a storage unit.

I sorted through the mess, piece by piece, until the room began to take shape again. As I worked, there was something oddly therapeutic about turning the chaos into order. The apartment slowly transformed from a forgotten, dusty relic into a place where I could at least catch my breath and plan my next move.

That's exactly what I did—I went to sleep, and as I drifted off, I realised that this apartment could be more than just a temporary refuge. It could be a base of operations. I was in a new country, with no real connections except for an international drug cartel that had generously provided me with a place to stay. They could probably help me out with narcotics as well, but I knew I had to tread carefully.

When I woke up the next day, I decided to reach out to my brother, Calle. We hadn't seen each other since I was crashing at Lurifilur's place, and I figured it was time to reconnect. I sent him the address, and when he arrived, things took a turn I wasn't expecting. As soon as he stepped into the apartment, he gave me a solid beating and demanded to know where his money was.

Oh, I remember now—I wasn't alone at the time. There was a guy named Murphy, an American I'd met on Istegade, who was also staying at the apartment. We had bonded over our shared situation, both of us essentially homeless and scraping by on the streets. Murphy was on his own version of a "vacation," but it was clear that the only thing he was really doing was getting high.

Calle, however, wasn't interested in Murphy. He sent him packing without a second thought, and then all of his anger was directed at me. As the reality of the situation hit me, I started to cry. We didn't even talk things out— there was no discussion, no attempt at understanding. He was high, furious, and he seemed to have forgotten that I'd had about 80,000 kronor taken from me. I simply didn't have the 36,300 kronor that I owed him for some hash and ecstasy.

Or maybe he was just pissed that he had to travel to another country to track me down. I don't really know what was going through his head, but I knew better than to mention that we were in a cartel-owned apartment. I had no idea how he would react to that, so I kept my mouth shut and just told him that I was planning to live in the apartment from now on.

It was a difficult moment, realising that the connection with my brother had deteriorated so badly. But I had no choice but to move forward and make the best of the situation. This apartment was now my base, my refuge, and perhaps my last chance to start rebuilding some semblance of a life.

Later that evening, the apartment door opened unexpectedly, and two cartel associates walked in without any prior notice. One of them was the man who had originally given me the key to the place, but the other was someone entirely new to me—a large, imposing figure whom I will refer to as T. His presence immediately changed the atmosphere in the room.

T didn't waste any time with formalities. He introduced himself and then casually dropped over 100 grams of cocaine and another 100 grams of heroin onto the living room table. It was an overwhelming amount, far more than I had ever handled before. Out of sheer curiosity and a bit of bravado, I tried a line of cocaine right off the tip of T's knife. It hit me harder than anything I had ever experienced—this was some seriously potent stuff.

T then asked if I could move the product and take it on credit from him. It was a straightforward proposition, but one that carried a lot of weight. I saw it as an opportunity—a chance to establish myself in the drug trade on Istedgade through this direct link to the cartel. I quickly agreed, sensing that this was a pivotal moment for me.

However, my brother, Calle, wasn't as eager. He immediately voiced his concern, saying there was no way he could let me take that amount on credit. As my older brother, he felt responsible for me and wasn't about to let me dive into something this risky alone.

"It's better that I take it on credit," he insisted, trying to take control of the situation.

But the man who had given me the key—my original Danish link to the cartel—pointed directly at me. "This is the man I know," he said. "Give it to him."

It was clear that they had come to help me out, recognising how far I had fallen. There was no discussion about the exact price or weight of the substances—they simply dropped it on the table, trusting me to handle it. It felt strange that I didn't bring up any of the old conversations I had had with the Swedish cartel associates. Perhaps I had forgotten them, or maybe I was just too focused on the new opportunity in front of me— selling coke and dope on the streets of Istedgade.

As I looked at the pile of drugs on the table, I couldn't help but think it was a shame that Murphy had been sent away. He could have been a valuable asset in this operation, a foot soldier on the streets. But that ship had sailed.

T, sensing the tension between me and Calle, stepped in. "It doesn't matter who takes the substances on credit," he said, his voice calm but firm. "You're brothers, and you're doing this together."

His words hung in the air, reminding us both that we were in this together—whether we liked it or not.

I found myself cooking up the cartel's coke into freebase on a metal spoon, using ammonia and a lighter. The process was precise—1 gram of powder turned into 0.93 grams of pure, potent freebase. It was 93% pure cocaine, and it hit like a freight train. The potency was unreal, almost too good, and I found the immediate risk of falling into a dangerous habit.

One of my favourite songs, "Ten Crack Commandments" by The Notorious B.I.G., echoed in my mind, particularly Rule #4: "Never get high on your own supply." But that wisdom slipped through my fingers as I indulged. I ended up smoking way too much, about 10 grams out of the initial 100. The euphoria was too tempting, too easy to chase, and before I knew it, I was deep in my own product.

Despite the setback, I had to keep the operation running. The cartel wasn't the type to forgive mistakes, and I needed to make sure we could move the product and make a profit. My brother and I, though at odds earlier, found a way to divide the labour. He took charge of watching the house, making sure everything stayed secure, while I hit the streets, hustling to move the product.

Being out on the streets, I was in my element. I knew how to navigate the underworld—making connections, finding customers, and dealing with the constant threats that came with the territory. But the weight of what we were doing hung heavy over us. Handling cartel substances wasn't just another street hustle; it was serious business, with serious consequences if things went wrong.

Despite the chaos and risk, the life I led on the streets brought a strange sense of vitality. The adrenaline rush from the hustle, the intense highs of the cocaine, and the constant dance with danger made me feel more alive than I had in a long time. It was a feeling I craved, even as I knew I was playing a perilous game. Every move was a step along a razor's edge, and any misstep could send everything spiralling out of control.

H17, the government-sanctioned facility, became our unlikely base of operations. The irony wasn't lost on me—selling substances provided by an international cartel within a place designed to offer safety and support to drug users. It was a twisted turn of fate, but it worked for us. The facility provided cover, a sense of community, and a place where we could operate with minimal scrutiny.

Power napping under the tables became a necessity in this life. My associate, Broman, and I took turns running the operation, selling rocks to a constant stream of customers. When it was his turn, I'd rest—closing my eyes, focusing on my breathing, and trying to shut out the world for a brief moment. Broman's only priority was getting his hands on cheap rocks, and he'd earn his share of free product with every sale he made. For every 500 he earned, he'd pocket a 150mg rock.

This system worked for us. It was a grind, but it allowed us to maintain a steady flow of business and keep our heads above water. We hustled day in and day out, navigating the underbelly of the city, making connections, and keeping the cartel satisfied with our progress. Broman would take his turn resting under the table, just as I had done, and we'd switch back and forth, keeping the operation running smoothly.

Looking back, I can see how entrenched we became in that life. The routine, the rush, and the constant pursuit of the next high were all-consuming. It was a cycle that fed on itself, and even as I knew I was teetering on the brink, I couldn't pull myself away. I'm sure Broman is still there today, chasing the same highs, entrenched in the same hustle, unable to break free from the grip of the life we had built.

Eventually, I grew tired of being my brother's puppet and reluctantly cut ties with him. It was clear that a business partnership wouldn't work between us when we couldn't even maintain a decent friendship.

Before becoming his drug runner, he'd used me as a punching bag. It was a far cry from the bond we once shared. The physical and emotional abuse completely shattered our relationship, which could have been incredibly profitable.

I found myself homeless, drifting from place to place. No amount of drugs could lure me back to him. During this time, I started using Tinder and eventually met Rikke Lund Olsen, who was kind enough to let me stay at her place occasionally. I was incredibly grateful for her kindness.

Rikke was a breath of fresh air. She was different from the girls I'd usually encounter. She was kind, understanding, and seemed genuinely interested in me. With her, I felt a sense of peace I hadn't experienced in a long time.

At some point, I arrived at Dortheavej 61, a youth house in Copenhagen that hosted a cooking program where the community could come together to prepare and serve meals to others. I found the atmosphere lovely and started frequenting the place. During one of my visits, I overheard that the youth house was also a gathering spot for Magic:

The Gathering players, which piqued my interest. I decided to show up on a Tuesday and was welcomed into an incredible Magic community.

I introduced myself to the group, explaining my homeless situation and how I had sold all of my Magic cards in Sweden, despite playing for roughly ten years. One of the kind players, whom I believe was Morten Humme, lent me a deck, and we bonded over our shared interest in Teferi.

Every Tuesday, I looked forward to these gatherings, where we would usually play Commander from evening to morning while enjoying cannabis. It was a splendid community that I truly treasured, providing a sense of belonging and a break from the challenges I was facing.

I also started visiting Malmö more frequently and became a regular at the cannabis stand run by two brothers, Babylon and Virre. They listened to my story and offered me a helping hand, starting with free weed and then gradually involving me in their operation. I ran errands, restocked supplies, and acted as a general assistant. Their kindness and generosity were a lifeline. Soon, I was spending most of my days at Malmö, helping them out in exchange for meals and a sense of belonging.

Before I knew it, I was a full-fledged member of their team, earning a substantial 2000 DKK a day. My responsibilities grew to include everything from security to sales. Eventually, they entrusted me with transporting multiple kilos of cannabis daily. It was an incredible turnaround from my life on the streets.

My first day as an employee was wild—I ran from the police twelve times, including one instance where I was transporting 2.5 kilograms of cannabis. It was exhilarating, and I couldn't help but find the whole experience incredibly amusing. It was the most hilarious job I had ever had, and the community surrounding it was fantastic. Both Babylon and Virre were super nice and treated me well. During that time, I either slept at the shelter on Hillerødgade or at Rikke's place.

Before I realised it, the handlers at Hillerödgade alongside Mission had put in work in order to get me off the streets—the commune recognised that someone as young as me shouldn't be living on the street, and they placed me in a group housing project. I was assigned to a room at Rådmandsgade 60, which I shared with two others. One of my roommates sold me a brand-new Samsung S7 Edge for 2000 crowns—a phone that cost 10,000 brand new. It was an incredible deal, likely because he took out a subscription and sold the phone as he needed money quickly.

My days were a blur of working in Malmö, biking back home, and stashing kilos in a locked duffel bag, one strap tucked securely under the foot of my bed. Life had taken an unexpected turn, but amidst the chaos, I found a strange sense of belonging and purpose. I owe a lot to the brothers for helping me out during my toughest days. Babylon, the older brother, asked me if I had a safe spot to put my money, but I unfortunately told him I didn't require any assistance with stashing my dough. Looking back, if I had asked him to keep it for me, I could have saved up a lot of money.

During my stay at Rådmandsgade, known as RG60, I met a lot of interesting people, but none as impactful as Mark Lange Jensen. A top bloke, Mark listened to my creative entrepreneurship plans and joined me in designing a rolling paper company.

We started by researching available suppliers of rolling paper. We ordered a sample box containing over 50 different types of rolling paper packages, all for $50—a deal I managed because my name apparently carried some weight in China.

I reconnected with my brother, who had initially been out of touch. Upon hearing about our entrepreneurship plans, he suggested we name the company "BestBuds." We loved the idea, so we registered two domain names: BestBuds.se and BestBuds.dk.

I also included my good friend William Svensson in our venture. William is a super intellectual, computer-savvy type who brought valuable tech expertise to our startup. With our combined skills and creativity, we were excited about the potential of our new business venture.

We ordered and tested several different products for our website, which was still under construction. One of my personal favourites was an electronic waterpipe. I dream of launching a website dedicated to selling these waterpipes one day.

During the startup phase, I continued working in Malmö. In hindsight, I regret not involving the Paradise team more. I should have encouraged them to assist with the startup rather than just mentioning it to them in passing.

How did things ever work out with the cocaine business that we started up running with the cartel? Well, to be frank, it was my initiative and thus my responsibility.

I left the responsibility on my brother, whom weren't able to manage it and when I got back in touch with him again, he needed my help in order to talk with some of the operatives that we/he owed the money to. They told him, "We can't believe that you would show your face without bringing any money."

"Don't you understand that we easily could bring something from the car in order to do something to you?"

"When are we getting our money?" My brother starts to say that he has a lot of friends that require hash and that he could pay off the debt that way. They tell me: "We will communicate with you seeing as your brother isn't stable enough, is it true?" I simply state that I have some money on the way from the commune and that the amount will be paid retroactively and I will thus be able to pay up a fair amount to them.

As time progressed, so did our website, work folder, and everything else associated with the project. Along the way, I met some amazingly talented rappers who could see themselves promoting our operation. Imagine them on stage, tossing out free rolling paper packages to the crowd.

That would truly be proper marketing.

Perhaps one day, if this book takes off and I accumulate a crowd willing to take part in the project, I could release all the data regarding BestBuds to the public. I could see myself doing that.

The events unfolded faster than I could process. It wasn't long before I got caught with two and a half kilos of cannabis. I found myself in the back of a police car surrounded by four officers. The tension was palpable as one of them punched my details into their system. The silence was broken by a voice that cut through the heavy air: "He has an active Interpol investigation." One officer remained tight-lipped, while the others exchanged glances, murmuring, "We didn't know that." Even now, I still wonder about the nature of that Interpol investigation. Was it due to my ties with international networks or a deeper association with criminal enterprises that had reached beyond borders?

The outcome of that arrest was swift and severe. I received a *zoneförbud* in Malmö, a strict ban that prohibited me from being anywhere near Pusher Street and the surrounding area where our stand operated. Common sense would have told me to stop, but I was beyond caring. This was my life, my team, my world—I wasn't about to throw in the towel just because of some restrictions and warnings.

But fate caught up with me again. It was a busy day, one of the few I'd taken off to breathe and escape the chaos. That was the day Malmö fell under full lockdown. Police swarmed the area, sealing it off with bandages and tape, their presence suffocating. I found a hiding spot in the "Greenland's Embassy," an old shelter known for providing refuge. I stayed silent and low, the tension in my muscles tightening with each passing second. But before long, the police burst through the doors, their heavy steps echoing off the cracked walls.

The closest officer approached without hesitation. His grip was iron as he yanked me up, spun me around, and cuffed my hands tightly behind my back. The cold bite of the metal dug into my wrists, each click of the cuffs sounding like the finality of a closing door. The weight of my choices pressed down on me, every reckless decision replaying in my mind. Regret gnawed at me, but defiance burned alongside it, an old flame that refused to go out.

They marched me outside, where the cold air stabbed at my face like needles. Malmö was no longer the haven I knew; it had transformed into a battle zone under siege. The familiar scents of weed and laughter had been replaced by the clinical hum of police radios and the raw edge of tension.

The ride to the station was suffocatingly silent. I sat in the back of the van, feeling every bump in the road, the gravity of the moment sinking deeper with each jolt. Would they punish me more harshly for refusing to cooperate? My decision to stay silent suddenly felt like a mistake—an impulsive move that could cost me more than I anticipated.

The station was a blur of harsh fluorescent lights and monotonous, muffled voices. I was processed, photographed, and led into a cold cell that smelled of old sweat and faded desperation. As I sat on the hard bench, staring at the chipped paint on the walls, the full weight of my predicament hit me like a tidal wave. This wasn't a warning or a minor consequence. This was the start of something much more severe—prison bars, court hearings, and an uncertain future hanging in the balance.

They had drone-surveillance footage of me handling cannabis, indisputable evidence that tied me directly to the operation. The trial was swift, the sentence delivered with little room for hope: six months in prison followed by a six-year deportation. As the judge's words settled over me, I sat in the courtroom, numbed by the finality. Denmark, a paradox of freedom and peril that I'd come to call home, was slipping away from me. This chaotic life I'd built, filled with both danger and moments of triumph, was being stripped away, piece by piece painfully.

I landed in a prison named Vestre Fangsle where I winded up snorting ADHD pills, smoking hashish and playing chess with Russian Mafia members.

When I first set foot in Vestre Fængsel, the iron bars and echoing corridors were a harsh reminder of my new reality. The cold, clinical environment quickly set the tone—survival here meant more than just staying physically safe; it required maintaining a sense of presence and dignity. The metallic clang of doors and the murmur of voices in different languages filled the air, underscoring the stark nature of this place.

Despite the intimidating atmosphere, I gradually found a rhythm. The prison housed people from all walks of life, each with their own story and hardened edges. There was no communal area except for the prison yard where we walked, so social interactions were limited to our cells. It was in these cramped, dimly lit spaces that I found myself drawn to games of chess. The Russian mafia members were particularly skilled at the game. They played with a cold, calculating intensity that mirrored their reputations. Their eyes narrowed with each move, and conversations were minimal, interrupted only by sharp, knowing glances or a smirk when a trap was set.

One afternoon, sitting in the narrow space of Ivan's cell, I watched as he moved his queen with a decisive flick, sealing his opponent's fate. He turned to me with a smirk. "You play?" he asked, his accent thick but his English sharp. I nodded, feeling the pulse of anticipation mixed with caution. That marked the beginning of my time at the board, learning not just the strategies of the game but how to navigate the complex dynamics of prison life.

Outside of these games, life in Vestre Fængsel had its own rhythm. Hashish was a valuable commodity, traded and smoked during the quieter hours when guards were less vigilant. The scent lingered faintly in the air, a fleeting reminder of freedom and familiarity. I found myself joining in, rolling and sharing joints with a few trusted inmates. It was a ritual, an escape that brought a brief sense of normalcy.

ADHD pills were also passed around as a means to sharpen focus or speed up the long, monotonous days. Snorting them in the confines of a prison cell felt surreal— a desperate grasp for control in a place where control was a rare luxury. The rush of the pills made time blur, temporarily dulling the edges of our reality.

Trust was scarce in Vestre Fængsel, and every interaction came with unspoken rules. Alliances were built slowly, their stability fragile. One day, after a particularly tense game, Ivan leaned back and fixed me with a serious look. "Prison isn't just these walls. What you do here follows you out," he said, his voice low but pointed. The weight of his words hung heavy, a reminder that even here, my choices would echo long after I left.

The days blended into weeks, marked by routine and punctuated by moments of tension and fleeting relief. I learned to read people's intentions in their gestures and to listen more than I spoke. Vestre Fængsel taught me lessons the streets never could: patience, the value of silence, and the true weight of consequence.

When I finally stepped out of Vestre Fængsel after three relentless months filled with self-reflection, self-hatred, and countless daily chess matches, the outside world felt both familiar and foreign. The bright daylight hit my face like a forgotten memory, sharp and blinding. Clutching my large, transparent plastic bag stuffed with the remnants of my prison life—letters, a few personal belongings, and that invisible weight of experiences—I set off for Gothenburg.

The train ride felt surreal, the hum of voices and the rhythmic clatter of wheels on tracks providing a backdrop to my jumbled thoughts. Each mile carried me further away from the grey, suffocating walls of the prison and closer to a world that felt slightly out of reach. I was free, but not unburdened.

When I arrived in Gothenburg, the fresh air filled my lungs and a wave of emotion surged through me. My cousin was there, waiting with a wide grin and open arms, embodying the warmth I had missed so dearly. He had arranged a pool party to welcome me back—a moment to cleanse the past few months and submerge myself in the joy of family and friends. The sight of the shimmering water, the laughter echoing around the yard, and the familiar faces hit me with a rush of relief. It was as if the weight of confinement finally loosened its grip, allowing me a moment of reprieve.

Amidst the celebration, I spotted Mission, my best friend, weaving through the crowd to meet me. His smile was genuine, the kind that reassured me that some things hadn't changed. As we embraced, I felt a surge of gratitude and nostalgia. Mission had always been a constant, a reminder of who I was beyond the mistakes, the deals, and the prison walls.

The evening passed in a blur of splashing water, shared stories, and the sweet, fleeting taste of freedom. For the first time in months, I felt the corners of my mouth lift in an unguarded smile. Yet, even as I laughed with Mission and my family, a part of me knew that the journey was far from over. The road ahead would be lined with challenges, but that night, surrounded by people who cared for me, I allowed myself a moment of peace. It was a small victory, but a necessary one, reminding me that even after the darkest chapters, life had a way of offering glimpses of light.

After spending all my saved cash on wild nights and endless parties in Gothenburg, I found myself returning to Y-town with nothing but the clothes on my back and the weight of my choices. The thrill of freedom had faded, replaced by a hollow emptiness and the gnawing reality of being broke. It was then that I made my way to my mother, Pia's house. I had missed her warm, home-cooked meals that carried the taste of comfort and familiarity.

The reunion was bittersweet. There were tense moments, conversations laced with disappointment and concern. Pia's eyes, full of worry, scanned my face for any signs that I was ready to change. I assured her that I would be different this time—I promised to be good, to stay out of the drug trade, and to live like a civilised man. I spoke with conviction, trying to convince her, and perhaps even myself, that I was ready to leave the chaos behind.

But promises, especially those made in desperation, can be fragile. It didn't take long before the restlessness crept back in. The quiet life felt suffocating, the allure of the fast lane and the rush of "the game" called to me louder than ever. The streets, with their whispers and opportunities, became impossible to ignore.

I remember vividly the night it all cracked open again. I was out with my friends, Oliver and Sebastian, lounging in the confines of their car, the air thick with nostalgia and mischief. We talked and joked, but before I knew it, the words slipped out of my mouth: "Are you guys interested in moving some kilos?" There was a brief silence, the kind that shifts the atmosphere and marks a moment of change. They looked at me with eyes that mirrored my own excitement and hesitation.

It was then I realised that despite my promises, I was still addicted to the thrill—the game that had a hold on me so deep that no amount of good intentions or second chances could break it. The promise I made to Pia felt like a distant echo, drowned out by the pounding heartbeat of the life I knew too well and couldn't stay away from.

Soon, I found myself back in the game, slinging hashish to my old clientele, carefully catalogued in my trusty Google Sheets list. My supply came from none other than William, the younger brother of my childhood friend Gustav—the same William I was working with on BestBudsAB. His small operation moved about half a kilo of hashish a month, and I pitched in by helping meet both his and my own clients' demands using his batch.

It didn't take long for William's supply to dry up, and I decided to take the reins and re-up. With 30,000 SEK from William in hand, I set out to procure a fresh kilo. This time, I bypassed my usual connections, Ragnar Vanheden and Charles Ingvar, in favour of a bigger player—a notorious drug lord who was known to supply even Ragnar and Charles. It felt like a bold move, but the promise of a solid return was too tempting to pass up.

The instructions were simple, or so I thought: drop the cash at one location and pick up the goods at another. The drop-off went smoothly; I handed over the money to an Arab contact in Lund, feeling a mix of nerves and anticipation. But when I tried to reach out to William Rosenberg, the drug lord, through Snapchat to confirm the pick-up, I realised I had been blocked. My pulse quickened as panic set in.

With the cash vanished and no drugs to show for it, I made a swift decision and headed straight to Ragnar. Desperation gnawed at me as I approached him, explaining that I needed to "credit" a kilo from him as a last resort. The plan was to somehow sort it out between both him and William, hoping I could clarify that I had been directed to pick up the hashish at Ragnar's place due to the separate pick-up arrangement mentioned by William.

During this period, my mother stumbled upon a freezer bag with a ripped-off corner in the trash. It was a tell-tale sign—evidence of me stashing 5 grams of hash, twisting the bag, and tearing it off for packaging. She called me over with a stern but concerned look in her eyes.

"I found this," she said, holding up the bag. The silence that followed was deafening. She didn't need to say much more. Her voice softened, but the disappointment was clear. "I'm sure this is drug-related. I can't have this in my home. I need you to leave."

Her words hit me hard, like a cold slap of reality. I felt a rush of emotions—shame, regret, and a touch of defiance—all swirling inside me. But I knew she was right, so I packed my suitcase, gathering what little I could carry, and left the home that had always been a place of comfort and warmth.

With nowhere else to turn, I reached out to my friend Ronja Lönnmarker and asked if I could crash on her couch for a while. She agreed without hesitation, her voice steady and reassuring. That simple "yes" felt like a lifeline, a small mercy in the chaos I'd created. I left my mother's house with a heavy heart, knowing that my choices had not only cost me a home but had also deeply hurt the person who had always been there for me.

I found myself in a small suburb just outside Y-town, the kind of place where the streets were quiet, and the air carried a sense of stillness. As soon as I dropped my bag by Ronja's couch, I sat down, already reaching into my pocket for my rolling papers and stash. Rolling a joint had become second nature to me; it was almost ritualistic, a way to reassert a sense of control and familiarity in my ever-chaotic life.

Within minutes, the scent of fresh cannabis filled the room as I expertly twisted the joint, each movement precise and practised. It was part of who I was, part of the image I had built for myself—the guy who always had the best weed and rolled joints that were the envy of any circle. The first inhale burned slightly, but the calming sensation that followed was instant, washing over the tension in my body and making the cramped space on Ronja's couch feel a little more bearable.

I glanced around her small living room. This was my new reality, a temporary refuge far from the comfort of my mother's home. Despite everything, there was a strange, fleeting comfort in lighting up that joint— a momentary escape from the weight of disappointment and the uncertainty that loomed ahead.

During my stay at Ronja's place, the atmosphere was unexpectedly comforting. We spent the first couple of days unwinding, surrounded by the soft glow of her cosy living room. The hum of the TV and the familiar sounds of our favourite playlists playing in the background created a sense of nostalgia that we both needed. We caught up on good old times, reminiscing about moments we'd shared before life became so complicated.

For two days straight, we binge-watched Netflix shows, switching between thrillers and comedies that kept us laughing until our stomachs hurt. The room would fill with our shared laughter, a brief escape from the world outside and the chaos that seemed to follow me everywhere. We'd pause episodes just to share stories sparked by the scenes, recalling wild nights and inside jokes that only we understood.

The smell of takeout and the faint aroma of my rolled joints added to the laid-back ambience. It was as if, for those fleeting moments, the weight of my current troubles could be pushed aside. The simple act of lounging around with an old friend felt like a reminder of a time when life was easier and my path less dangerous.

Yet, beneath the surface, there was an unspoken tension. The silence between conversations was heavy with what neither of us dared to bring up—the unresolved mess waiting for me once this brief respite came to an end. But in those moments, we let ourselves sink into the comfort of music, Netflix, and the company of an old friend, grasping for whatever peace we could find.

During this time, I maintained my connections and kept up appearances within my circle. I remember vividly the conversations I had with Sammy Bolin during this period. We planned to meet up in Kristianstad just three days after I'd settled in at Ronja's place. The anticipation of seeing Sammy again gave me a fleeting sense of normalcy amid the chaos.

When the day arrived, I brought Ronja along for the trip to Kristianstad. The ride was filled with casual chatter, but there was an underlying tension as my mind kept circling back to the unresolved situation with William Rosenberg and the hash I had credited from Ragnar. Despite the uncertainty, I needed to show that everything was under control, even if it was just a facade.

Once in Kristianstad, we met up with Sammy and a few of his friends—two men from Syria and another from Lebanon. The atmosphere was friendly but had a certain edge, as it always did when unfamiliar faces were involved. We lit up joints rolled with the hash from Ragnar's batch, the smoke curling into the cool afternoon air as laughter and stories flowed.

After a while, I explained the predicament I was in, outlining the deal gone wrong with Rosenberg. Sammy listened intently, nodding along, while one of his friends leaned forward and offered me an unexpected lifeline. He suggested I rent his apartment for 5,500 SEK a month. It was a modest place, but it promised stability—something I desperately needed at that moment.

Without hesitating, I agreed to the deal. The arrangement felt like a fresh start, a chance to recalibrate and sort out the mess I'd found myself in. After finalising the details, I returned to Ronja's to gather my belongings. I thanked her sincerely for giving me a place to stay when I had nowhere else to go. As I packed up my things and prepared to leave, a mix of relief and anxiety coursed through me. I was stepping into a new chapter, but the weight of unresolved debts and uncertain alliances loomed heavily in the background.

Kristianstad (2019)

After a period of drifting, I found myself in Kristianstad, managing to secure an apartment. It wasn't much, but it offered a semblance of stability. The landlord, Sammy, seemed easygoing, and before long, I was regularly smoking hash with him, alongside Yousef and Ibbe—two Syrian refugees who had made a name for themselves in the local scene.

For a brief moment, I thought I had found a haven. The air in the apartment was thick with smoke and laughter as we passed joints and shared stories late into the night. But my optimism was short-lived.

One evening, the landlord orchestrated a setup. Without much warning, I found myself face-to-face with William Rosenberg and a few others. Their demands were clear: they wanted the kilo of hash I had credited from Ragnar. The confrontation was intense, with tempers flaring and threats hanging in the air. Under the crushing weight of peer pressure and the looming threat of violence, I reluctantly agreed to work off the debt.

The arrangement was straightforward—or so it seemed. They would provide me with hashish and amphetamine to sell, but I quickly realised the operation wasn't as professional as they had claimed. My first "delivery" was washing powder, dropped off by a man on a bike who casually tossed the bag ten metres ahead of me.

I had thought I was dealing with heavy players, but this farce made it clear they were anything but. The landlord's betrayal, coupled with the faux product, left me vulnerable and constantly on edge. The fear of being assaulted lingered with every moment I stayed in that apartment.

It didn't take long for me to decide that staying was no longer an option. I packed a hand-baggage and made my way to the airport, leaving Kristianstad behind. Whatever awaited me in Belgium couldn't be worse than the volatile mess I was leaving behind—or so I thought.

Belgium (2019 - 2020)

The flight to Belgium felt like an escape, a final attempt to distance myself from the chaos that had unravelled back in Kristianstad. The tension was palpable as I sat in my seat, mind racing, while the muted hum of the engines provided a strange kind of comfort. Before boarding, I had hastily ditched my snus can stuffed with tramadol, tossing it into the bushes near the airport entrance. Paranoia gnawed at me as I replayed the moment, wondering if the gamble was worth it.

Sliding through the messages on Snapchat, my pulse quickened as I re-read the landlord's threats. His anger bled through every word, warning me that my belongings would be thrown out if I didn't respond. Clothes, electronics, sentimental items—everything I had accumulated over a month or two of living in that cramped apartment in Kristianstad now dangled in limbo. But I couldn't risk replying. The threats, the sudden shifts in tone from people I once trusted—it all felt like pieces of a larger scheme, something I couldn't quite put my finger on but feared all the same.

The cabin lights dimmed as the plane descended, and I nursed the drink in my hand, hoping the alcohol would dull the sharp edge of my anxiety. When we touched down, I braced myself for customs, expecting a gauntlet of questions, stern looks, or perhaps worse. Instead, there was nothing—no security checks, no customs officers scrutinising passengers. I walked through without so much as a glance from an official, the ease of it almost laughable. A bitter chuckle escaped my lips as I realised I could have kept my tramadol after all. That final sting of regret settled in, the irony burning just as hot as the fear I had felt only hours before.

"Fucking hell," I muttered under my breath, the weight of everything catching up to me. The uncertainty of what came next loomed large, but for now, at least, I was in Belgium.

Arriving in Leuven after a restless bus ride from Brussels, I stepped into a city that felt both foreign and familiar. The cobblestone streets glistened under the soft glow of streetlights, whispering stories of history and intrigue. The uncertainty of my situation gnawed at me, but I was driven by the need to reconnect with the cartel and reclaim my place in a world that felt distant after my time in prison.

With a duffel bag slung over my shoulder, I approached a passerby and asked for a recommendation on where to get a drink. He nodded and pointed me toward Café Belge, situated in the main square. The café exuded warmth with its wooden interiors and a crowd buzzing with conversation, providing a strange comfort after the sterile coldness of a cell.

As I stepped inside, I noticed two men in sharp suits seated at a corner table. They stood out from the casual crowd, their presence commanding attention. Both were covered in tattoos that peeked out from beneath their cuffs and collars, intricate designs that told stories of lives lived on the edge. One of them was Jesper Verplanken with a shaved head and who was full of tattoos just like the other, Leks (May he rest in peace), who had a shaven head decorated with an array of ink, adding to his formidable presence.

Jesper's sharp eyes met mine, and he extended a hand as I approached. "Jesper Verplanken," he introduced himself, his voice steady and cool. Next to him, Leks leaned back, arms crossed, his gaze unwavering.

"Fresh out of prison, I hear," Leks said, the corners of his mouth curving into a thin smirk. His voice carried the weight of someone who knew more than he let on. I took in the tattoos that adorned his arms and neck, intricate pieces that seemed to blend seamlessly into the larger canvas of his scalp. Both men were not just cartel associates but skilled tattoo artists whose art told tales as bold as their lives.

I nodded, sliding into the seat they offered. "Yeah, it's been a rough stretch. But I'm here now."

Jesper listened intently as I laid out my situation—my fresh release, the need to reestablish connections, and the uncertainties that still loomed. Leks's eyes never left mine, his expression unreadable but focused.

"We've been expecting you," Leks finally said, his tone hinting at familiarity and command. "There's a room ready for tonight. Rest up—you'll need it."

Relief washed over me, loosening the tension that had knotted my shoulders for weeks. For now, I had a place to stay and allies whose inked skin and sharp eyes promised stories as deep and dark as the path I was about to walk. The road ahead was uncertain, but it was mine to reclaim, and at this moment, that was enough.

I went up to Lek's apartment, located on the opposite side of Café Belge, still overlooking the lively main square. The air was filled with the ambient hum of conversations and the occasional laughter drifting in from the streets below. The familiarity of the sounds outside contrasted sharply with the newness of my surroundings. It felt reassuring, a brief reprieve from the chaos that had followed me for months.

As I stepped inside, the apartment had a warm, lived-in feel. The eclectic mix of modern furnishings and old-world charm made it an inviting space. I found the sofa in the corner of the living room, bathed in the soft light of a streetlamp filtering through the curtains. It wasn't much, but to me, it felt like a luxury—a place to rest and breathe without glancing over my shoulder.

I dropped my bag beside it and stretched out, letting my body sink into the worn cushions. The exhaustion of the past weeks started to wash over me, the adrenaline that had kept me moving finally giving way. I made my makeshift bed on the sofa, using my jacket as a pillow and a blanket that had been folded neatly on the armrest. For the first time in what felt like forever, I allowed myself to close my eyes, listening to the muted sounds of the square, and drift into a sleep that I desperately needed.

The very next day, when I awoke, I took a moment to orient myself, the early morning light casting a soft glow across the room. I gathered my thoughts, deciding that I needed to get a sense of my surroundings. I left my few belongings—a modest bag with the essentials—safely at the apartment and stepped outside, eager to explore Leuven.

The city welcomed me with its vibrant, historic charm. The cobblestone streets were lined with old buildings adorned with intricate facades, each telling its own story. I wandered through narrow alleyways that opened up to bustling squares, where locals sipped coffee at café terraces and bicycles whirred by with effortless speed. The scent of freshly baked bread mingled with the crisp, cool air, sparking a sense of curiosity that had been dormant for far too long.

I found myself drawn to the heart of the city, where the towering spires of the Town Hall stood as a testament to Leuven's rich past. It was a mix of Gothic splendour and the hum of modern life that resonated with me. For a moment, I could almost forget the chaos that had brought me here, and I allowed myself to simply exist—an outsider blending into the rhythm of a city that moved with an ease I hadn't known in years.

As I explored Leuven, I quickly tapped into the city's pulse, finding the places where the nightlife was vibrant and the crowds were always ready for a good time. It didn't take long before I spotted the perfect opportunity in local social clubs like Rumba. These were places where people came to lose themselves in music, neon lights, and the fleeting connections of the night.

Having solid cartel connections in Rotterdam, I managed to smuggle in quantities of MDMA and ecstasy. The trips were always a curious blend of nerve-wracking and exhilarating. I'd meet my cartel associates in a dimly lit café, where deals were finalized under the guise of casual conversation. We'd laugh, take photos for Instagram, their faces obscured with animal head emojis to maintain anonymity. It was a strange juxtaposition: the light-hearted social media posts masking the darker undertones of our dealings.

Transport was never straightforward. After picking up the goods, I'd change cars multiple times before heading to the FlixBus station. The route was risky, a patchwork of caution and calculated moves. Hidden compartments in my bags and meticulous planning helped avoid detection, but the adrenaline of crossing borders with contraband in tow never faded. The hardest part was not the smuggling itself, but maintaining an air of calm once I had safely made it to Leuven.

Rumba, along with other social clubs, became the heart of my new operation. The energy in those places was electrifying—pulsing lights, thumping bass, and crowds that seemed to vibrate with life. The clubs provided the perfect backdrop for my trade, where subtle nods and quick exchanges were easy to make amidst the chaos. My clientele was a mix: university students looking for a break from their relentless studies, and regulars who knew where to find the highest quality.

Word spread quickly. The MDMA and ecstasy I sourced from Rotterdam were top-tier, and soon enough, I had a steady flow of customers. Each night was a balancing act between risk and reward, with the stakes rising as my reputation grew. The thrill was undeniable, but so was the awareness that one wrong move could unravel everything. The thin line I walked between success and disaster grew sharper with every deal, leaving me both exhilarated and haunted by the potential fallout.

I eventually cemented my commitment to the cartel by getting a tattoo on my left arm—spanning nearly its entire length—that spelt the name "Sinaloa" backwards. Interestingly, when I later searched it, I discovered that "Aolanis" was also a Hawaiian name. But to me, it was a symbol of loyalty and allegiance: Sinaloa becoming Aolanis, tied together in ink and meaning. The thought behind this was to be able to deny a connection to the cartel if ever asked about it.

Shortly after, I met up with Jordan, one of my most consistent buyers who frequently purchased in bulk.

When we met at his apartment, he immediately noticed the fresh tattoo peeking out from under my sleeve. His eyes widened with curiosity, and he leaned forward, "Is that real?" he asked, the disbelief clear in his voice.

I nodded without hesitation, the memory of the needle's bite still vivid. For a moment, there was silence, broken only by the faint sounds from the street below. Then Jordan's expression shifted; respect mingled with awe. He reached out for a firm handshake, solidifying not just our deal, but an unspoken bond. "From now on, I'll always re-up from you," he said, a declaration of loyalty and trust now backed by the knowledge that I was directly connected to the cartel.

The tattoo served as more than just a mark; it was a testament to the stakes I was willing to accept. It drew a line in the sand, marking my deep dive into a world where trust was rare, and loyalty was everything. The risks were high, but with each acknowledgement of my affiliation, the influence I wielded grew, embedding me further into the complex and perilous network of the trade.

At some point, I met a fellow named Bram (may his soul rest in peace), who was deeply immersed in what he called "the arts"—smoking cocaine. Drawn by both curiosity and the allure of new experiences, I joined him, and soon we were performing this ritual together regularly. Bram had a certain energy about him, a chaotic charisma that made it easy to get swept up in the reckless abandon of those nights. The room would fill with thick clouds of smoke, our conversations drifting from deep reflections to uncontrollable laughter, all while the world outside seemed to blur and fade away.

Not long after, I managed to convince my brother, Calle, to come over. He hesitated at first but eventually agreed to take a flight and join me. When Calle arrived, he was immediately thrust into the intense lifestyle I had built—a blend of camaraderie, danger, and indulgence. It felt surreal having him there, a piece of home amid the unpredictable reality I had embraced in Belgium.

I truly appreciated Calle taking the flight from Denmark. It meant more than I could express, knowing he was willing to step into this chaotic chapter of my life just to be by my side. His presence brought a sense of familiarity and grounding, a reminder of where we came from and the bond we shared. Having him there added a layer of comfort amidst the storm, even as we found ourselves swept up in the unpredictable and dangerous lifestyle I had carved out.

Calle's arrival was like a silent pledge that no matter how far we strayed from normalcy, we were in this together. The late nights, the shared laughter, and the reckless choices felt a little less isolating with my brother next to me. He didn't judge or question; he just stepped into my world and adapted, bringing a sense of loyalty that kept me anchored, even as the boundaries of right and wrong blurred around us.

When Calle arrived, he suggested I try signing up for some 9-5 work to keep myself occupied during day-time and bring in legitimate income. Taking his advice, I went to Flying Kitchen, an agency that placed workers in different kitchen jobs. However, I quickly realized that I needed a Belgian bank account to proceed. I reached out to Bram, who, true to his helpful nature, offered his account for me to use. With that sorted, Flying Kitchen assigned me to various kitchen roles almost immediately.

By day, I was scrubbing down kitchen areas, cleaning dishes, and occasionally chopping vegetables or assisting chefs with basic prep work. It was humbling work, grounding me in routine and providing a stark contrast to my double life. By night, the streets called me back, and I resumed my dealings, supplying ecstasy and MDMA to local clubs and social circles. The juxtaposition was surreal—spending my daylight hours as an ordinary kitchen aid, lost in the clatter of pots and the sharp tang of dish soap, only to step into the pulsing nightlife where I slipped back into the role of a dealer. The days were long, blending into nights, and while the work was tiring, the duality gave me a strange sense of balance amidst the chaos. We moved from place to place, never staying too long at any one location. Some nights were spent at friends' apartments, where couches became our temporary beds, while other nights found us crashing at various squats around the city. It was an ever-changing cycle, a rotation that kept us moving and gave our days a sense of unpredictability. The constant shifting meant adapting to new environments, new faces, and a continuous stream of introductions and goodbyes.

Each spot had its own character—some offered warmth and camaraderie, with laughter echoing late into the night and shared meals scraped together from whatever was available. Others were colder, lonelier, where silence spoke louder than words, and the nights felt long and restless. Despite the instability, we learned to embrace the rhythm, finding comfort in the routine chaos. The variety kept us sharp and aware, but it also carved a deeper sense of longing for something more permanent, more secure.

The three of us—Calle, Joshua, and I—set out on a mission to find a more permanent place to call home. Joshua, one of the many Italians we'd met during our time in Leuven, quickly became part of our makeshift family. He had an infectious laugh and an easy-going attitude that lightened even the most stressful days. We shared stories late into the night, swapping tales of our pasts and dreams for the future over smokes and drinks.

The search for a stable residence was not easy; Leuven's housing market was competitive, and landlords often raised an eyebrow at our unconventional trio. We combed through listings, attended viewings, and hustled for leads, all while balancing our patchwork lives of work and street business. Each place we looked at came with its own set of challenges—one apartment was too cramped, another too far from the heart of the city, and others simply unaffordable.

Despite the obstacles, we kept our spirits up, knowing that finding a place of our own would mean more than just a roof over our heads. It would symbolize a bit of stability amid the chaos, a safe space where we could regroup, rest, and plan our next moves. Joshua, with his network of Italian friends, often found us leads and vouched for us when necessary, making it feel like the goal was within reach. We knew that once we secured a place, it would be the foundation for a new chapter, one where we could regain a sense of normalcy, even if just for a little while.

Looking back, we had a tight-knit group of Italian friends who became like family—Joshua, Dino, and Alberto, each bringing their own character into the mix.

Dino, in particular, was a true gentleman. I still remember the times he'd come to pick me up, always standing beside his small Fiat with both the driver's and passenger's doors open, waiting for me. He'd greet me with a classic Italian kiss on both cheeks, a gesture that made me feel welcomed every time.

Dino's floor became my unofficial accommodation just as Alberto's did. Crashing on their floors was far easier on my budget than spending on hotel rooms every night. Those shared spaces felt more like home than any rented room could, filled with laughter, late-night conversations, and a strong sense of camaraderie that kept us going, no matter where the day took us.

I vividly remember that period when I'd started snorting stimulants again—primarily cocaine, though occasionally amphetamine. I had somehow landed a job washing dishes at a Volvo car expo, and the setup was almost surreal. Every night, I'd crash on Dino's floor, a setup that was comfortable enough for both of us to keep losing track of time. On one particular morning, we overslept, and Dino, in true Italian fashion, decided to make up for it by pushing his little Fiat to its limit. We sped down the 80 km/h road to Brussels at over 120 km/h, a tablet of amphetamine on the dash, which I pressed toward his nose as he drove, both of us riding a dangerous high.

When I finally got to the expo, a bit late, I was dressed in a full suit—ironic for a dishwashing gig, but I'd received more than a few compliments that day. Some of the car salesmen even joked that I looked more polished than they did, which added to the thrill of the whole experience. Between rounds in the kitchen, I'd sneak off to the bathroom, re-upping with lines of cocaine, blending the adrenaline rush of the job with the edge of the high. It was, in the strangest way, exhilarating; I even took a few pictures for Instagram, though the exact duration of that job is a bit of a blur now. That whole period was fast-paced, risky, and, looking back, incredible that I'm here to tell the story.

Leuven had become a strange mix of adventure and unpredictability, my days divided between late nights at clubs and the grind of whatever odd job I could land. The car expo job at Volvo was a particularly surreal experience, almost like playing a role in a movie scene I never auditioned for. Every morning, Dino would be there, standing by his little Fiat with both doors open, cigarette dangling from his lips, ready to tear down the highway to Brussels if we'd overslept again.

One crisp, hazy morning, Dino leaned against the car, watching me through a cloud of smoke. "Today, Hugo," he said, flicking the ash, "you're not a dishwasher. You're a man of mystery. A gentleman among the dishpans." It was his way of saying, "Fake it 'til you make it."

Inside the expo, people noticed the suit right away. Some laughed, others whispered, and I caught a few sidelong glances from the salesmen on the floor, as if sizing me up for competition. When I took my breaks, I'd find a secluded bathroom stall, a quick line of coke to sharpen the edge, a splash of cold water on my face to stay steady. It was almost a ritual, a way to center myself in this fast-paced, reckless life I was carving out.

Outside of work, life took on its own rhythm. I'd split my time between Dino's place and crashing with other friends, like Alberto and Joshua. The Italian crew was always rotating locations, squatting here, renting a place there. Joshua was a character—one of those guys you could meet once and feel like you'd known for years. He'd share whatever he had, and somehow, it felt like a real family.

Then, there was Rumba, the club scene, where I found a certain thrill selling to the crowds. It was almost like a second job, one that felt more natural in the dim lights, with bass-heavy music that made everything feel urgent and alive. The business started picking up speed, too, and the danger only made it more thrilling. Every night felt like a tightrope walk between success and catastrophe.

But there was another side to it all, a kind of numbness that crept in after a while. Nights stretched into early mornings, the exhaustion settling deep. One evening, back at Dino's, he noticed. He looked at me, really looked at me, his usual joking manner replaced with a rare seriousness.

"Hugo," he said, "you're in this deep. Are you even sure where you're going?"

For the first time, I didn't have an answer, just a shrug, and a silent realization that the path I'd chosen was barely a path at all—just a series of decisions stacked one on top of the other, with no end in sight. The thrill, the rush, the camaraderie—it was all real, but somewhere beneath it was a quiet question I didn't want to answer: *How long can this last?*

Eventually, what no one could have foreseen occurred: the entirety of Leuven went into lockdown due to a virus known as COVID-19. My brother and I found ourselves holed up in a squat—a small, half-decayed cabin tucked deep in the woods outside Kessel-Lo. The city's bustling streets were replaced by the rustling leaves and the muffled silence of the forest, a complete shift from the life we'd been living. Our only neighbour was Pico, a once-famous Belgian actor who had grown old and reclusive, wrapped up in the shadows of his past and an addiction that had long since taken hold. Despite the haze that seemed to cloud his days, he had a kind side. He'd often stop by our cabin with little stories of his acting days, or a record he thought we'd appreciate.

With nowhere to go and few people left around, our rotation of friends and associates evaporated into the quiet. The cabin became our entire world, its walls filled with the smell of forest dampness, and the soundscape dominated by bird calls and Pico's occasional laughter or, on other nights, silence heavy as stone.

Life in the cabin was surreal. The thrill of city life and its chaotic nights had vanished, leaving us with firewood, chilly evenings, and an eerie sort of peace in the middle of a global storm. We spent nights talking around a fire we made out back, sometimes joined by Pico. He'd let slip a few stories from his prime—moments we'd later replay in our minds when the silence of the woods seemed too thick. Those forest days stretched on, a strange chapter that felt like it didn't belong to anyone but somehow, for a time, belonged to us.

Isolation took its toll. Days bled into nights, and the constant confinement, with only the echo of our own thoughts and each other's company, began to weigh heavily on both of us. Tensions that were once manageable deepened, and eventually, Calle drifted off for days at a time, leaving me alone in the silence of the cabin.

One evening, the loneliness grew unbearable. In the cabin's shadowed stillness, I found a rope and tied it to a sturdy wooden beam. I slipped the noose around my neck, the weight of everything feeling almost suffocating. I stood there for a moment, the rough fibres against my skin as the hollow quiet of the forest pressed in on all sides. The feeling was haunting, yet it was somehow grounding, bringing a sort of clarity that hadn't come in weeks.

I took the rope off, leaving it where it hung, and went to find some paper. Instead of giving in, I left a note on the rough wooden table, scribbling down my plan: I would head to Brussels Central Station, and I'd wait there for Calle, hoping he would come. We'd go together to the embassy, seek help—anything to break this pattern. I folded the note and set it on the table, gathered my things, and, with no hotels open and nowhere else to go, made my way out of the cabin in the woods and toward the road that would lead me back into the world. The woods around me were silent, only the faint rustle of leaves echoing in the air, making the isolation feel even more absolute. The thought of Brussels station, a place bustling with life and motion, was somehow comforting. It offered an escape from the oppressive stillness that had grown between Calle and me, the silence that spoke louder than any argument we could have had.

The decision to wait for Calle at the station was my last grasp at reconnecting, or maybe just escaping the dark thoughts that had crept in over the past few days. The isolation had torn at both of us, but perhaps more so at me, I thought as I walked out of that cabin and into the damp, chilly air of the forest. I began the journey with nothing but a small bag slung over my shoulder, carrying only essentials. The first part of the trek was winding and muddy, my boots sinking slightly into the damp ground with each step. My mind replayed memories of the highs and lows of the past few months—my hasty arrival in Belgium, the odd jobs, the faces of friends and strangers, the chaos and thrill, the precarious balancing act.

When I finally reached the outskirts of Leuven and saw the sign pointing toward Brussels, a flicker of relief came over me. As the miles slipped by, each one brought me closer to a glimmer of hope that maybe things could shift, that maybe Calle and I could find some sense of normalcy, even if it meant starting over entirely.

Arriving at Brussels Central was like stepping back into reality. I found a spot just off to the side of the station entrance and sat down, clutching my bag. The city pulsed around me, the hum of people, the occasional call for a train arrival, the sounds of life moving forward. I waited, watching the faces that passed by, looking for the familiar one I hoped would appear. The city felt like a ghost town. Brussels, usually bustling with life and energy, was eerie in its silence. With the military patrolling and almost no civilians in sight, I could barely recognize the place. I set up a makeshift camp just outside the central station, a strange sanctuary in an isolated world. Food drops became my lifeline—people in masks would come by, quickly setting down boxes of supplies before moving on without a word. It was surreal, but that rhythm of small daily interactions kept me grounded in some strange way.

One day, as I was tearing open one of these food boxes, I noticed a figure standing off to the side, watching. He was unmistakably Italian, with a slight swagger that seemed both confident and weathered. We struck up a conversation, and it turned out his name was Salvatore Capone, recently released from prison and trying to piece things together in a world that had changed overnight. We ended up sharing the food, both of us wary yet drawn to the odd companionship that came from navigating such an unusual time.

In a world empty of familiar comforts, Salvatore and I became allies. There was something refreshing in his straightforwardness; he wasn't interested in small talk or pretence. Each day, we'd gather around our makeshift spot, sharing food and swapping stories from our pasts, and figuring out how to survive in a city overtaken by silence and uncertainty.

Over the days, Salvatore and I found a rhythm. Each morning, I'd scout the station's perimeter while he held down the fort, securing what few belongings we had stashed. There was a shared understanding that went beyond words—we were both survivors, and now, we were surviving together.

One night, as we sat in silence under the pale glow of the streetlights, Salvatore broke the silence. He shared pieces of his own story—a mixture of hard decisions and regrets, punctuated by a stint in prison that left him with a hardened edge. For him, this post-lockdown Brussels was just another prison, only this time, it wasn't four walls keeping him in; it was an entire city.

Salvatore had his own contacts, and soon enough, we discovered ways to make a little cash. People still wanted certain things, virus or not, and the isolation had only heightened the demand for them. Small deals were made in quiet corners, and the station became our unofficial base. We managed to scrape by, navigating the strange half-life of the city together.

Days bled into weeks, and the surrealness of it all became the new normal. Salvatore introduced me to a few other hidden spots around Brussels where small groups would gather, defying isolation, sharing cigarettes, and exchanging stories. It was in these spaces that I felt the weight of everything—the danger, the uncertainty, the strange thrill of the life I had carved out here, almost on the fringes of society itself.

One evening, Salvatore mentioned a plan—he wanted to return to Italy once the restrictions eased. The thought of losing this unexpected friend hit harder than I expected. The reality of my own situation loomed: what was I even waiting for here, camped outside a train station, dodging soldiers and curfews?

In those moments, I felt a strange kinship with the ghostly streets of Brussels—a city as locked up as I felt inside.

With Salvatore Capone as my unexpected new companion, life took on a surreal edge as we adapted to the new rules of the world. Salvatore was fresh out of prison and seemed as lost in the post-pandemic city as I was. Though the streets of Brussels were quiet, an unspoken tension hummed in the air—like everyone was holding their breath. Between the military presence and empty streets, we lived like shadows, drifting around the city's edges, trying to avoid attention.

Our routines grew strange, like something out of a half-baked survival novel. During the day, we'd wander around, scoping out new drop-off spots where charities left food or hygiene products for people in need. At night, we'd retreat to makeshift spots where we could sleep without fear of getting pushed along by the authorities.

Salvatore, despite everything he'd been through, had an almost unfathomable optimism. He'd tell stories of his life before prison—his family in Italy, the seafood dishes his mother used to cook, and the coastline he missed with an almost tangible ache. His perspective was a strange comfort, a reminder of life beyond the confines of the city and the pandemic. It was an irony that wasn't lost on either of us: here we were, two people society had already written off, yet here we were, surviving together in the middle of Brussels.

One afternoon, as we sat by a fountain, Salvatore looked over at me, the usual grin slipping from his face for a moment. "What will you do, once this is over?" he asked.

The question hit like a weight. What was I going to do?

It dawned on me then that I'd drifted far from my original mission of heading to the Embassy for help. The plan had been simple enough: find some sort of transportation home and, with any luck, reconnect with my brother and leave this chaos behind. But the days had a way of stretching on, and survival became the only mission.

During the lockdown, a few shelters opened up makeshift hygiene stations for those of us still left wandering the streets. La Fontaine was one such place. There, you could shower, get your clothes washed, and even store a few belongings. It was a small sanctuary, a place that offered some semblance of normalcy. I left a suitcase there, packed with whatever essentials I'd managed to hang onto—and strangely enough, it's probably still sitting there to this day, a relic of those strange, suspended times.

Each visit to La Fontaine felt like a brief window back into humanity. The staff would hand out clean clothes and meals, and for a few minutes, I could almost pretend things were normal. But once I left those doors, the quiet, empty streets were there to remind me that normal had long since left Brussels.

Every now and then, I'd find myself thinking about the Embassy and that original plan. I'd imagine Calle and me finally walking through the doors, getting our paperwork sorted, and boarding a plane home. But something kept me here—maybe the thought of facing everything I'd left behind or the slim hope that something would shift if I waited just a bit longer

.Calle's arrival in Brussels felt like a breath of fresh air, cutting through the heaviness of isolation. I had settled into a kind of routine, but seeing his familiar face reminded me that we still had something real to hold onto. As soon as he dropped his bags, we set out for the usual spots I had discovered, making our way to the steps outside the station where people sometimes gathered to swap stories or, like us, just pass the time.

That's where we met Seppe. He was a local with an easygoing grin and an almost uncanny ability to blend in, knowing everyone and everything about the streets of Brussels. Alongside him was Salvatore Capone, the Italian I'd met recently. He was fresh out of prison, with stories as heavy as the bags under his eyes, yet always game to join in on whatever distraction we could think of.

Calle, Seppe, Capone, and I found ourselves in a game of bottle flip, using whatever half-full plastic water bottles we could get our hands on. It started out light, each of us trying to one-up the other with the most creative flips—a spin, a backwards toss, landing it on steps, even balancing it on ledges. The stakes climbed with every round. Calle's competitive edge kicked in, and he was relentless, taunting Capone, who, despite his gruff demeanour, was surprisingly good at the game. Seppe, the local king of street games, was all flair—flipping with extra spins and fancy tricks that had us laughing and cheering like kids.

Capone leaned into the game with a kind of fierce dedication, muttering Italian under his breath whenever a flip went wrong. He'd narrow his eyes, refocus, and nail the next attempt. It was oddly comforting to see how a simple game could pull us all together, bridging languages and backgrounds. In those hours, we weren't just people thrown together by circumstance but a makeshift crew, each bottle flip feeling like a small triumph over the loneliness of the lockdown.

As the day turned into night, we kept playing, laughing louder as the station lights flickered on. That night, Brussels didn't feel so empty; it felt like a place we could call our own, if only for a little while. The morning after our bottle-flipping marathon, Calle and I made the decision to finally head to the embassy. It was a place of last resort, somewhere I'd initially resisted, clinging to the hope that we could tough it out a little longer without having to seek official help. But as the days wore on, the uncertainty of our situation pressed down on us. So, with our few belongings slung over our shoulders, we made our way through the quiet streets to the embassy.

The walk was almost surreal. The normally bustling avenues were ghostly, with an occasional military patrol rolling by, casting long shadows on the empty sidewalks. The embassy itself was unassuming, blending in with the old architecture of Brussels. A couple of guards stood outside, masked and distant, eyeing us carefully as we approached.

Inside, the building was a strange mix of formal efficiency and unease. The waiting room was eerily quiet, with only a few others scattered around, all of us spaced out and masked, sharing the unspoken tension of being far from home in the middle of a global lockdown. After what felt like an eternity, a woman with a calm, practised voice called our names, gesturing for us to follow her into a small office.

The consul, a no-nonsense man with grey hair and an almost apologetic look in his eyes, listened as I explained our situation. I tried to keep it simple, mentioning only the essentials—that we had been stuck here since the outbreak, had no secure place to stay, and were barely managing.

As we stood in the embassy, the consul surprised us with an option we hadn't anticipated. "We can arrange a flight back home for you immediately," he said, looking up from his paperwork. "However, if you'd prefer, we could set you up with a flight in the next few weeks, giving you time to get your affairs in order here."

Calle glanced at me, and I could tell we were both weighing the decision carefully. There was a part of me that wanted nothing more than to get out of Belgium, to leave behind the months of struggle and uncertainty. But I also knew that this meant wrapping things up quickly and saying goodbye to the strange yet grounding rhythm we'd found in Brussels.

Taking a deep breath, I asked for a moment to talk it over with Calle. We stepped outside into the chilly air, the silence between us heavy with the choice at hand. We talked about the people we'd met, the temporary sense of community we'd somehow pieced together, and whether it was wise to stay in a place where our future felt so uncertain. There was something about having a few more days to make peace with our time here that felt strangely important.

After a few moments, we walked back in and gave the consul our answer.

Calle had made up his mind and wanted to leave at once. Calle and I walked down to the station in silence, the noise of the bustling central station surrounding us. He was focused, intent on getting his suitcase, and I couldn't help but feel a mix of pride and sadness. Calle had always been decisive, practical, and there was something reassuring in watching him make the choice so clearly. He was ready to return home, to leave the chaotic months in Belgium behind.

At the storage lockers, Calle grabbed his suitcase and turned to me, giving me a long look. "You're sure you want to stay?" he asked, his voice calm but with a note of worry underneath. I nodded. "There's still something here for me, I think," I replied, not fully convinced myself. But it was true—something about staying in Belgium felt unfinished, as if I was on the edge of building something real here. We'd been so close to setting up a full operation, a place, even people who knew our names. And while that came with its own risks, it also felt like an opportunity I couldn't walk away from just yet.

Calle put a hand on my shoulder, a rare gesture of affection from him. "Alright then," he said, "But you know where to find me."

As he turned to leave, I watched him disappear into the crowd, a lone figure navigating his way back to a life we'd almost left behind.

After Calle's departure, I soon found myself deeper into the life that had quickly become my new norm. Not long after he left, someone stopped by with about twenty grams of heroin, and I took it as if it were a casual favour.

I went and gathered the tools I'd need to inject it, slipping into the routine I had fallen into, a hazy escape from reality.

One night, while in the middle of this familiar ritual, something jolted me back. A commotion broke out close by. I glanced over and saw a girl, a regular around these parts who often slept outside, struggling against a man. For a split second, the fog lifted, and I could see the threat clearly in her eyes. Instinct kicked in.

I rose from my sleeping bag, adrenaline overriding the numbness in my body. I strode over and, before I knew it, I had him in a chokehold from behind. I felt the tension in his body as he tried to resist, but I tightened my grip, pulling him away from her. A minute went by, maybe more, before I loosened my hold and when I did BAM.

The fog lifted gradually, giving way to stark white walls and the sterile beeps of machines around me. My arms felt heavy, and as I moved, I realized they were tethered with tubes, needles sticking out at strange angles. It was a hospital bed, that much was clear, and the figures around me were speaking rapidly in French, their voices laced with shock. They hadn't expected me to be conscious.

I tried to piece together the fragments of what had happened, each memory a half-formed thought. Six days.

I had been out for six days. It was hard to reconcile—the last clear moment in my mind was the chokehold and the rush of adrenaline. I'd stood there, finally letting go, and then... darkness.

One of the nurses, wide-eyed, moved closer, whispering quickly to a doctor as she glanced in my direction. Though their words were indistinguishable, the concern on their faces spoke volumes. I was confined to a wheelchair, utterly dependent on the hospital staff for even the most basic tasks. My head had been shaved, leaving a sterile patchwork of scalp exposed, a stark reminder of the emergency procedures that had saved my life.

Whenever it was time for a shower, nurses would carefully carry me, their hands firm but gentle, as though afraid I might break. I felt like a shadow of myself, every ounce of autonomy stripped away, and the effort of simply existing was overwhelming.

The reality hit me hard: I had narrowly escaped death. I had suffered a brain haemorrhage, and the doctors later told me I was mere minutes from losing the battle altogether. I owe my life to Capone, who had acted swiftly, calling for medics when I was left battered and broken, essentially stomped to death in the chaos of the streets.

Those first days blurred into a haze of pain, silence, and introspection. The knowledge of how close I had come to the end was both terrifying and strangely grounding. I started asking myself questions I hadn't dared to face before: *Why am I still here? What is the purpose of this second chance?*

The hospital's cold sterility became my world. I began to find solace in small moments—the brief smiles of the nurses, the rhythmic hum of machines, and the warmth of sunlight filtering through the windows. Despite the despair of my condition, I couldn't shake the feeling that this was some kind of turning point, even if I didn't yet know which direction I was supposed to take.

I had only my coat with me, the pockets carrying my only lifelines: my passport and the numbers for both my father and mother scribbled on the back in case of emergencies. They had already been contacted, and the news of my condition had started to ripple outward. When I finally got access to my social media through an iPad the institution loaned me, I was floored to see a GoFundMe page in my name. My sister had set it up, aiming to raise enough money to pay for a helicopter to bring me back to Sweden, given that all flights had been cancelled due to the ongoing Covid lockdowns.

It was a strange, sobering moment to see my life laid bare for strangers to judge and potentially save. The donations trickled in—small amounts from people who knew me, bigger ones from family and friends. The comments ranged from heartfelt prayers to casual words of encouragement. Despite my fractured state, I felt gratitude, even if part of me hated needing help at all.

Axel Wiberg, my old gaming friend even donated 500 SEK to the cause. I was moved.

Dino came to visit me not long after I got back online. As always, he was an anchor in the chaos, but his arrival carried its own storm. He stepped into the sterile hospital room, his familiar swagger somehow out of place in the clinical setting. His first words weren't about my health or my survival; they were a question steeped in vengeance.

"Do you want me to burn down their house?" he asked, his tone casual, as if it were an everyday offer.

I couldn't help but chuckle at the absurdity of it, even though part of me knew he was serious. "No, Dino," I replied, shaking my head. "That's not the answer."

But Dino being Dino, he didn't come empty-handed. Along with his usual charm, he brought me a small stash of ketamine, hidden discreetly in his jacket. The sight of it felt almost surreal against the backdrop of the stark hospital room. It was a reckless gesture, but one that spoke of loyalty in its own twisted way.

That night, under the veil of darkness, I waited until the ward was quiet before indulging. I went to the bathroom, snorted a line of ketamine, and stared at myself in the mirror. My reflection was haunting—a shaven head, hollow eyes, and a face that had seen too much. Yet, there was a flicker of defiance in my gaze.

"Yo soy un hombre de Sinaloa Cartel," I shouted to myself, the words both a declaration and a reminder. They echoed in my mind, blending bravado with despair. I didn't fully believe them, but in that moment, they gave me a sense of control, however fleeting.

I stumbled back to my hospital bed, the world tilting on its axis as the drug took hold. The cold reality of my situation was momentarily replaced by a haze.

I stayed in the hospital for what felt like an eternity, though I can't recall exactly how long. Time seemed to blur as one day bled into the next, marked only by the sterile routine of nurses, checkups, and the faint murmur of hospital life. My memories from that period are hazy at best, but there's one thing I remember vividly—a big act of support from my mother, she was always looking out for me. Somehow, she managed to wire money to the hospital. The staff withdrew it on my behalf, ensuring I had a little bit of comfort amid the monotony. With those funds, I indulged in simple pleasures that felt almost extravagant given my circumstances—Belgian waffles, warm and sweet, a fleeting escape from the hospital food, and rolling tobacco to occupy my restless hands.

It was a strange ritual, savouring those waffles and carefully crafting each cigarette. In the absence of normalcy, these small moments felt grounding, even comforting. The sweetness of the waffles reminded me of better days, while the ritual of rolling tobacco gave me something to focus on—a semblance of control in an otherwise uncontrollable situation.

Even in my disconnected state, I felt a faint glimmer of gratitude. It wasn't just the waffles or the tobacco—it was the reminder that, despite everything, someone out there still cared enough to send a piece of the outside world into my fractured one.

The day my mother and brother, Carl-Axel, arrived to pick me up was surreal. I had been floating through a fog of pain, recovery, and detachment for so long that seeing their familiar faces brought a strange mix of relief and unease. They had come to take me home, to Sweden, despite the doctors' clear warnings against leaving so soon. My brain haemorrhage was no small matter, and they insisted I should stay for further observation and care.

But I was done with the hospital. The sterile walls and relentless routine had drained me. I craved the open road, familiar surroundings, and some semblance of normal life. So, against medical advice, I packed up what little I had left—mostly rolling tobacco, a handful of notes scribbled on loose paper, and the clothes Dino had brought me— and left with them.

Their car was a fancy lease vehicle, a sleek symbol of their determination to bring me back, paid for with funds raised through the GoFundMe page my sister had set up. I felt a pang of guilt, knowing that strangers and loved ones alike had chipped in to get me out of Belgium and back to Sweden. Yet, I also felt a quiet gratitude, though I didn't express it outright.

The journey home was a mix of emotions. As we crossed the border out of Belgium, I gazed out the window at the countryside blurring past, each mile taking me further from the chaos I had endured. My mother drove, whilst Carl-Axel sat next to her. Allowing me to lay down to get some rest in the backseat. I assured them both I was fine, though deep down, I knew my recovery was far from complete.

The hum of the car engine, the scent of my mother's perfume, and the faint sound of a playlist Carl-Axel had thrown together created an odd sense of calm. It felt good to be in their company, even if the road ahead—both literal and figurative—was uncertain. I sat silently, lost in thought, as we made our way back to Sweden, wondering what awaited me on the other side of this journey.

I would also like to add here that while I was in Belgium, one of my deepest regrets is postponing my visit to my brother, Christian, in France, where I had hoped to enlist his help in pursuing my goal of joining the French Foreign Legion. Looking back, I wish I had acted sooner, pushing that agenda before the COVID-19 pandemic disrupted everything and made traveling to see him impossible.

Despite the distance and the missed opportunity, Christian and I maintained our connection, even through some of the most challenging times of my life. After my brain haemorrhage, when I was hospitalized and struggling to piece my life back together, Christian was there for me in a way that truly showed his character and our bond as siblings. I'll never forget the day he sent me a laptop to use while I was in the hospital—a gesture that might seem small to some but was monumental to me. It wasn't just about the device; it was his way of showing that he believed in me, even when I wasn't sure if I believed in myself.

Christian's unwavering support and kindness during that period remind me of the importance of family and how vital it is to cherish the relationships we have. While I may have missed the chance to walk a certain path with him, I know the bond we share transcends missed opportunities. It's a reminder to act on what truly matters in life, while also appreciating those who stand by us, no matter the circumstances.

Sweden (Year 2020)

When I got back to Sweden, my mom insisted that I take her bed while she slept on the couch. I protested, arguing that I was fine with the couch, but my arguments fell on deaf ears. In her mind, the king-size bed was non-negotiable, and I was "forced" to enjoy its comfort. It felt almost surreal to lie there after everything—like being cocooned in safety for the first time in what felt like forever.

She had even gone the extra mile and bought me a brand-new gaming laptop. It was an incredible gesture that filled me with a quiet gratitude. I used it to finally dive into *Dragon Ball*—the original series. Despite being an avid anime and manga fan, *Dragon Ball* had always been one of those iconic titles I'd somehow never gotten around to watching. Lying in bed, wrapped in soft blankets, and following Goku's early adventures felt like a small but much-needed escape.

The next day, my mother and I headed to the hospital for a checkup on my injuries. The lingering effects of my brain haemorrhage and other complications still needed attention. Before I could even step inside, I had to sit in a COVID-19 testing tent, a stark reminder of the strange times we were living in. The staff, clad in protective gear, moved efficiently, but the atmosphere was tense.

While I waited, my mom snapped a photo of me sitting there, a mix of exhaustion and quiet determination on my face. That moment felt significant—a small snapshot of resilience after so much chaos. If we ever find that photo, I'm sure it'll make its way to social media, a relic of a chapter where survival was the primary goal.

That week in Sweden marked the beginning of a slow return to something resembling normality. It wasn't perfect, but it was a start.

After seeing the doctor, my mom and I headed to the Swedish Tax Agency (*Skatteverket*). The visit was necessary to officially document my stay at her address— a step to help me reestablish some semblance of stability after everything that had happened. It felt oddly grounding, walking into the sterile office and filling out forms, a bureaucratic process that reminded me I was back in the structured environment of Sweden.

In the days that followed, my best friend, Mission, came to visit me. His arrival was like a burst of energy, the kind only a close friend can bring. We laughed, reminisced, and spent hours talking about everything and nothing. For a while, it felt like old times, like the chaos and the pain of the past months had been pushed aside, even if just temporarily.

Mission had a knack for making even the simplest moments feel extraordinary. Whether it was grabbing a meal, playing games, or just sitting around swapping stories, he brought a sense of lightness that I desperately needed. Those few days together were a reminder that, no matter how dark things got, there were still pieces of my life worth holding onto.

As the months went on and my health improved, my mother gently suggested that it might be time to start thinking about my future. She had found the perfect place for me: Axevalla Folkhögskola, a school where I could not only study but also live on campus.

One sunny afternoon, I met up with Tuva, my old bestie, and her energetic dog, Kira, at the beach. It was a rare moment of serenity, the waves lapping against the shore as we caught up. She asked me what my next steps were, her eyes full of genuine care.

"I've decided to enrol in a campus," I told her, my voice steady but tinged with uncertainty.

Her eyebrows shot up in surprise. "Already? So soon after... everything?"

I nodded, explaining how my mother had found Axevalla Folkhögskola online and thought it would be a good fit. "It's a chance to study and stay away from all this. To get a fresh start."

Tuva listened intently, her thoughtful expression betraying a hint of concern. She didn't say it outright, but I felt she wanted me to stay in Ystad. And looking back, maybe I should have.

If I had stayed, I could have lived off sick leave benefits, gotten an apartment through the commune, and started BestBuds—my dream business. More importantly, I could have gotten proper treatment for my fractured skull. The idea of staying close to Tuva and the familiarity of Ystad now feels like the path I should have chosen.

But back then, I wasn't thinking clearly. The thought of continuing to burden my mother, living in her cramped apartment, was unbearable. I felt an urgency to leave, to start anew, even if it meant stepping into the unknown.

That day at the beach, as Tuva and I laughed about old memories and Kira darted around chasing seagulls, I realized how much I valued her presence. Her quiet strength and kindness had always been a source of comfort. A part of me wondered if leaving would mean losing that connection, but I buried the thought.

For now, Axevalla Folkhögskola felt like the right decision—or at least the one I convinced myself was right.

One day, Mission and I decided to hit the town and ended up booking a hotel in Malmö. We were having an amazing time, just living in the moment, when out of the blue, I got a message on Instagram from Nikita. She had spotted me at the hotel and was curious about what I was up to and whether I wanted to meet up. I couldn't believe it—we hadn't seen each other in eight years, not since my school graduation back in 2014. When we finally met, it was as if no time had passed at all. Everything just clicked into place; we held hands, kissed, and it felt like we had never been apart. It was like those eight years of distance melted away in an instant, leaving us right where we left off, still connected, still in sync.

Axevalla Folkhögskola (Year 2021)

After settling into Axevalla Folkhögskola, the student dorms quickly became more than just a place to rest—they transformed into the birthplace of BestBuds, and a hub of late-night creativity and camaraderie. While school was technically the reason for being there, I didn't see it as just attending classes. For me, this was an opportunity to finally launch my enterprise, to prove to myself and everyone else that I could create something meaningful and impactful.

The beginning was anything but ordinary. To mark the start of this new chapter, we threw a massive get-together. Drinks flowed, laughter echoed through the halls, and I even invited my best friend, Mission, who travelled six hours just to be there. The party was unforgettable, but not without its complications.

I found myself feeling remorseful after a fleeting moment with a 19-year-old girl named Anna. While that happened, Mission had gone off with Emelie and her boyfriend Rabi to their room, where an unfortunate incident unfolded. Emelie, in a drunken lapse, called Mission a racial slur. The words stung more than I could have imagined. Mission, a dark-skinned gentleman from Jamaica and one of the kindest souls I know, was deeply hurt. Seeing his pain was unbearable, and it reminded me of how destructive ignorance could be.

But amidst the chaos of dorm life, the vision for BestBuds began to take shape. This wasn't just about starting a business—it was about creating something positive that could benefit others while giving me a fresh start.

The idea of producing CBD and melatonin-infused e-liquid came during a late-night brainstorming session with my dormmate Nemo, a vaping enthusiast with a knack for problem-solving. Soon after, we roped in Jalil, a chemistry whiz, and Hussein, the dorm's charismatic social butterfly, to round out the team. The concept was ambitious: a vape liquid that combined the calming properties of CBD with the sleep-enhancing benefits of melatonin.

The dorm's communal kitchen became our makeshift laboratory. Jalil meticulously measured ingredients, experimenting with the formula while Nemo sourced vape cartridges and tools. Hussein kept spirits high with his unrelenting optimism, always ready with a joke or a pep talk when frustration crept in.

Our early attempts were far from perfect. The formula was inconsistent, flavours clashed, and the smell of our experiments wafted through the halls, much to the annoyance of other students. But each failure taught us something new, and we kept refining the process.

One memorable night, after what felt like endless tweaks, we nailed it. The e-liquid was smooth, with a refreshing minty flavour and just the right blend of relaxation and sleep support. We celebrated like we had just discovered fire, high-fiving and laughing until the early hours.

The name of the brand, *BestBuds*, was, and still is, a no-brainer. Back when we were brainstorming names over countless hours at Rådmandsgade, the process felt endless. We tossed around ideas, debated endlessly, and overcomplicated what should have been simple. Then, in true Calle fashion, my brother chimed in with his signature straightforwardness.

"Just go with *BestBuds*," he said casually, as if it were the most obvious choice in the world.

And he was right. It was perfect—a name that captured everything we wanted to stand for: quality, community, and the idea of being a trusted companion in both business and friendship. It clicked instantly, and from that moment on, *BestBuds* was more than just a name. It became the heart of what we were creating.

That's the reason why Calle, my brother will always be allowed to be a part of what I am building.

Nemo spearheaded the branding, designing sleek, minimalist packaging that oozed professionalism. Jalil ensured we included detailed product information to emphasize transparency, while Hussein crafted pitches to local vape shops and health stores. I took charge of marketing, ordering branded clothing—T-shirts, polo shirts, and bucket hats—along with a staggering 20,000 stickers for a guerrilla marketing campaign.

The Instagram account @BestBudsAB was created.

Of course, it wasn't all business. Dorm life had its own rhythm, full of shared meals, late-night chats, and impromptu adventures. We had movie nights where the common room became a makeshift theater, complete with popcorn and overly dramatic commentary. The kitchen wasn't just our lab—it was also where we experimented with cooking, often creating meals that were as chaotic as they were delicious.

One night, Hussein convinced us to try making shawarma from scratch. It was a disaster—we ended up with a charred pita and a kitchen full of smoke—but the laughter and camaraderie made it worth it.

We also spent time outdoors, exploring the surrounding area and occasionally venturing into nearby towns. These small breaks from the grind reminded us why we were doing this in the first place—not just to build a business, but to build something meaningful together.

I was required to take routine urine tests, given my well-known association with cannabis—a reputation that wasn't surprising considering I was in the process of launching a cannabis-based company. Though it felt intrusive at times, I understood the reasoning behind it. To my relief, I passed every drug test without issue, which helped to validate my commitment to BestBuds and a fresh start.

One of the most significant milestones for BestBuds was when I connected with Phil Huang, a sharp and meticulous businessman based in Xi'an, China. Phil had been following our progress on social media and saw potential in the concept of CBD and melatonin-infused products.

After a series of 5 a.m. video calls where we discussed product specifications, market potential, and logistics, Phil offered to translate the entire BestBuds website into Mandarin. It was no small feat, but he delivered with precision, ensuring that every detail—product descriptions, usage guidelines, and even our brand philosophy—was culturally and linguistically appropriate for the Chinese market.

Phil didn't stop at the website. He used his network to source high-quality melatonin and CBD for us, which significantly reduced costs while maintaining top-tier quality. His efforts opened up discussions about entering the Chinese market—a challenging but potentially lucrative move.

Around the same time, Toni, a charismatic project manager from California, joined our team. She had an impressive portfolio, having worked on various startups in the wellness industry. Her role in BestBuds was to streamline operations, align our goals, and, most importantly, help us navigate the labyrinth of international business regulations.

Toni's insight into branding and marketing was invaluable. She often emphasized the importance of creating a story around BestBuds—something that would resonate with consumers globally. "You're not just selling a product; you're selling a lifestyle," she said during one of our strategy calls. Her energy and optimism inspired everyone on the team to dream bigger.

The final piece of our international puzzle was Kim McCarthy, the owner of Pipeline Strategies, a well-respected product review platform in the cannabis industry. Kim was introduced to us through Toni, and after some initial conversations, he agreed to test and review our products.

We sent her a batch of our blunt cones, carefully crafted. A week later, Kim posted a detailed review on her platform, praising the smoothness, flavour profile, and overall experience of the product. "BestBuds has nailed the balance between quality and innovation," she wrote, adding that she saw the potential for the product to carve out its niche in an increasingly competitive market.

The dorm at Axevalla Folkhögskola became a hub of activity. Late nights were spent coordinating shipments, tweaking formulas based on feedback, and brainstorming marketing strategies. Phil's translations helped us tap into the Chinese market, while Toni worked on crafting a pitch for investors in California. Kim's glowing review gave us credibility in the industry.

These collaborations weren't just about business—they were about the connections we were building.

BestBuds was no longer just a dorm project; it was becoming a global endeavour.

Then, all of a sudden, in the middle of an otherwise quiet morning, I heard the news that Ragnar Vanheden's family house had been blown up. The blast had torn through the structure, leaving it a hollow shell of what it once was—a place of memories, warmth, and safety. My heart sank as I learned that all of Ragnar's siblings had been home at the time of the explosion. By some miracle, they had escaped unharmed, but the trauma of the event would undoubtedly scar them for life.

It didn't take long for whispers to circulate about who might be behind such an act of terror. All signs pointed to William Rosenberg. His fingerprints, though metaphorical, were all over this—his reputation for vengeance and control made it clear.

As the weight of the news settled over me, I felt my chest tighten with guilt. It was as though the blast had reverberated through my very soul, shaking loose the fragments of past decisions I'd made—or failed to make. Every choice, every moment of inaction, seemed to converge into this singular, catastrophic event.

Had I acted differently, could this have been avoided? I couldn't shake the thought that my own hand, indirectly, had played a part in this tragedy. The feeling was suffocating, an overwhelming cocktail of regret, responsibility, and helplessness.

As I stood there, grappling with the magnitude of what had happened, I realized this wasn't just about Ragnar or his family. This was about a ripple effect I had set into motion long ago—an intricate web of consequences I could no longer control. And now, innocent people were paying the price.

The destruction of that house wasn't just a physical act of violence. It was a message, a warning, and a symbol of the far-reaching consequences of choices made in a world where loyalty, power, and betrayal collided.

I knew then that I couldn't turn back the clock. But I also knew I couldn't ignore the role I had played in all of this. Somehow, I had to find a way to confront the chaos I had helped unleash, even if it meant facing the demons I had been running from for far too long.

Ystad

As the school year drew to a close, summer break approached and it was time for me to return home to Ystad. The dorm life had been a whirlwind of excitement, collaboration, and personal growth. The shared meals, late-night chats, and constant camaraderie made the student campus feel like a second home. But as much as I cherished those memories, a part of me yearned for independence.

I wanted to arrange my own living quarters—a space where I could focus solely on growing BestBuds and starting fresh, away from the distractions of campus life. The idea of having my own apartment was liberating. It symbolized stability and a step toward the future I was building for myself.

And so, I began the search for apartments. Each listing I browsed felt like a small glimpse into the life I wanted to create—a place to truly call my own, where I could merge my personal and professional ambitions seamlessly.

During the summer break, I shifted my focus toward fetching investors to elevate *BestBuds* beyond the confines of the dorm kitchen. Balancing this with living off Swedish study funds (*CSN*) was no easy task. Every krona was stretched thin between covering my basic needs and supporting the company's start-up expenses. Survival and ambition often felt like two sides of a coin, but I was determined.

Eventually, I got an invitation to an investment meeting in Stockholm. The person I was supposed to meet was Pehr—a man known for taking calculated risks and backing unconventional ideas. This felt like the opportunity I had been waiting for.

I gathered my belongings and prepared a comprehensive portfolio filled with all the necessary paperwork, financial projections, product samples, and branding mockups. The preparation felt surreal, almost like I was stepping into a role I had dreamed of playing for years.

As the day of the meeting arrived, I carefully packed my portfolio, ensuring nothing was left behind. With anticipation bubbling in my chest, I made my way to the train station and boarded the train to Stockholm. Watching the Swedish countryside blur past the window,

I couldn't help but imagine what this meeting could mean for *BestBuds*.

Would this be the break I needed to finally bring the vision to life on a larger scale?

Stockholm

Arriving in Stockholm felt like stepping into a new chapter. As soon as I got off the train, I contacted Vanessa, a girl I had met through the Swedish Facebook group known as AKC (*Avkriminalisera Cannabis*), which roughly translates to "Decriminalize Cannabis." Vanessa's writing stood out to me; she had a way with words, and I thought she'd be perfect for creating content for *BestBuds'* website.

We arranged to meet, and when we finally connected, we instantly hit it off. Vanessa was warm, intelligent, and full of life. Our day together was an absolute blast. We wandered through Stockholm, talking about everything from cannabis reform to creative writing, and it felt like we had known each other for years.

As evening rolled around, we headed back to the hostel where I was staying for the night. The city streets had quieted down, but outside the hostel, we encountered a man named Gustav. His dishevelled appearance and slightly frantic demeanour immediately caught my attention.

"Do you have any water?" he asked, his voice tinged with desperation.

Concerned, Vanessa and I went inside to fetch him a bottle. When we returned, Gustav studied us for a moment, as if gauging whether we were trustworthy. Then, almost casually, he confessed, "I've been injecting cocaine in the outdoor toilets nearby. I'm overheating."

The situation was surreal. I hadn't touched any substances in over a year and had been fiercely proud of that. Yet, as I stood there, a familiar itch began creeping up, accompanied by a gnawing sense of curiosity. My resolve wavered.

"Do you have any cocaine?" I blurted out before I could stop myself.

What followed was a whirlwind of poor decisions. Gustav shared his stash, and the three of us—me, Gustav, and Vanessa—ended up spending the entire night snorting cocaine. It was chaotic, messy, and reckless. Vanessa, perhaps wisely, opted out of most of the madness, retreating to my hostel bed while Gustav and I continued our binge.

By the time 5 a.m. rolled around, we were starving. With the last of my funds, I ordered pizzas for everyone, devouring them as if they were the best meals we'd ever had. Once the food was gone, the high had begun to wane, and reality started creeping back in.

We parted ways shortly after. Gustav disappeared into the early morning streets, while Vanessa and I headed back inside. Exhausted, I climbed the stairs and found her in the dorm bed. Without thinking, I hugged her from behind—a small, silent gesture of gratitude for her presence amidst the chaos. Then I collapsed onto the mattress and finally let sleep take me.

The very next day, I found myself trailing Vanessa to her place. She had offered me a quiet spot to work on the *BestBuds* website, and I was eager to regain some semblance of focus after the chaos of the previous night. I settled at her desk, typing away and trying to shake off the lingering haze. But peace is fleeting when you've already started down a destructive path.

Out of nowhere, one of her friends arrived, casually pulling out a bag of amphetamine-like it was a pack of chewing gum. My resolve, already weakened, crumbled completely. The slippery slope I had once climbed out of opened wide beneath me, and I willingly tumbled back into its depths.

"Well, trying it once won't hurt," I told myself, knowing full well the lies addicts tell to justify their decisions. But the amphetamine was garbage—weak, gritty, and disappointing. Yet, instead of walking away, it sparked an idea.

Fueled by frustration, I reached out to an old connection and placed an order: 20 grams of what I thought would be proper amphetamine for 999 SEK. It felt almost ridiculous not to round up to a full thousand, but every coin counted when you were trying to navigate the dark corners of the web. After the Bitcoin transaction was processed, I received confirmation that the package was being prepared and shipped directly to my hostel.

When it arrived, I eagerly tore it open, expecting the usual speed. What I found instead was a crystalline substance—methamphetamine. I stared at it, dumbfounded. This was a whole new level of dangerous, a drug I had always sworn I'd never touch. But the curiosity and the hunger for escape overtook me once again.

I made my way to a needle exchange, walking through Stockholm with a mix of shame and anticipation. The staff at the exchange gave me the sterile equipment without judgment, but their silent understanding weighed heavily on me. Back at the hostel, I locked myself in and prepared the first injection.

The high hit me like a freight train. My thoughts raced, my energy soared, and suddenly, nothing seemed impossible. Hours blurred into days as I binged on the meth, writing feverishly on the *BestBuds* website. Vanessa and her friend, drawn by the allure of my new stash, started buying from me as well. I became both a user and a dealer, trapped in a cycle of supply and demand.

I barely slept. My mind was a whirlpool of ideas and paranoia. The content I poured into the website was an endless stream of text, much of it nonsensical in hindsight. Pages upon pages of poorly thought-out plans, half-finished sentences, and ramblings that only made sense in the fog of my high.

And yet, in the midst of this chaos, something miraculous—or absurd—happened. Somehow, between the manic episodes and the chemical haze, I secured an investment of 90,000 SEK. To this day, I can't fully explain how I managed it. Was it charisma? Luck? Or did I simply catch the investor at a moment when my wild enthusiasm seemed convincing?

Whatever the case, the money was real, and for a fleeting moment, it felt like I had achieved something. But even with the funds in hand, I couldn't ignore the gnawing realization that my addiction was spiralling out of control.

The high points of *BestBuds* were beginning to clash with the dark lows of my personal life. I was teetering on the edge, juggling dreams of success with the self-destructive habits that threatened to ruin everything.

After securing the funds, I said good bye to Vanessa and thanked her for the pleasant times in Stockholm and headed back to Ytown.

Ystad

I was back in Y-town, baby! The small coastal city welcomed me with the same sleepy charm, but I was far from the person who had left it. I was injecting meth straight into my veins—always in the shower to rinse the blood away immediately—and celebrating my *BestBuds* victory like it was the biggest achievement of my life. Securing such an impressive investment felt like a vindication, a sign that my dreams were finally within reach despite everything I'd been through.

Amidst the haze of self-congratulation, more great news arrived: there was an apartment available for me in Ardala, just 10 minutes away from the school. It felt like fate. I had the funds to stabilize my life, a place to call my own, and my business plans were slowly coming together.

Ardala

I wasted no time heading to Ardala to finalize everything. The apartment was a humble two-bedroom with just enough charm to feel like a fresh start. I signed the paperwork with a sense of pride, imagining how I'd finally create a proper base of operations for *BestBuds*. That evening, I stood in my new living room, envisioning shelves lined with product samples and brainstorming strategies to expand my reach.

But reality, as it often does, came crashing down the very next day.

A call from the school shattered my fragile bubble. They informed me, quite bluntly, that I was being expelled. My cannabis business—despite my insistence that it was fully legal and focused on CBD—was reflecting poorly on the school. It didn't matter that I was working hard to make something of myself; all they saw was a scandal waiting to happen.

"You've brought unwanted attention to our institution," the administrator said coldly. "We can't have that."

I was stunned. After everything I'd poured into my time there, this felt like a betrayal. Sure, I hadn't been the most attentive student, but I was building something real, something meaningful. And now, with one swift decision, they'd taken away not only my education but also the community I'd found in Axevalla.

That evening, I sat in my new apartment in Ardala, staring at the lease agreement I'd just signed. It felt bitterly ironic. I had the space I'd wanted, the resources to start fresh, but the foundation I'd built it all on had been ripped away.

Still, deep down, I knew this wasn't the end. If anything, it was a challenge—a chance to prove that I didn't need anyone's approval to make my dreams a reality.

I picked up my phone and started drafting a plan. If the school didn't want me, fine. But *BestBuds* wasn't going anywhere. I'd turn this setback into an opportunity, just like I always had.

With my expulsion from Axevalla Folkhögskola, my focus shifted entirely to *BestBuds*. It was a bitter pill to swallow, being forced out of the very institution I thought would support me, but I wasn't about to let it stop me. I had an apartment, a vision, and the investment funds to keep pushing forward. If anything, this setback lit a fire under me to prove everyone wrong.

Interestingly, my brother Calle ended up enrolling at Axevalla after I left. It felt strange knowing he was there, walking the same halls I had, without ever really mentioning me. We were brothers, sure, but our paths rarely intersected in meaningful ways. He had his own life and priorities, and I was too caught up in my whirlwind of projects to dwell on it.

My neighbour, Björn, was a character in his own right. A rough-around-the-edges guy with a love for beer, air rifles, and spontaneous tattoos, he became an unlikely companion during my time in Ardala. On countless evenings, we'd sit outside, cracking open cheap beers and shooting at random targets with his air rifle.

One hazy night, Björn decided I needed some ink to solidify my dedication to *BestBuds*. With his shaky hands, he began tattooing the letter *B* on my right arm. The plan was to eventually spell out "BestBuds," but by the time the *B* was done, our mental states—clouded by alcohol—convinced us to postpone the rest. We never got back to it, and the lonely *B* became a quirky reminder of those chaotic nights.

Björn was also generous—or perhaps reckless— enough to let me borrow his motorbike whenever I needed to run errands. I didn't have a license, but he never asked, and I never told. Riding through the small roads of Ardala on that bike felt liberating, a momentary escape from the weight of everything else.

With the investment funds secured, I dove headfirst into expanding *BestBuds*. I set up a makeshift office in my apartment, complete with stacks of packaging supplies, bottles of CBD and melatonin concentrate, and a cheap printer for invoices. I'd sit at my desk for hours, juggling social media campaigns, responding to inquiries, and perfecting the product line.

I also started experimenting with new flavours for the e-liquids, using feedback from customers and friends. The dorm had been a great starting point, but now I wanted to scale up. I reached out to vape shops, wellness stores, and even a few influencers to help spread the word.

Despite the grind, I still found time to enjoy the little things. Some evenings, I'd ride Björn's motorbike to the store, picking up snacks and beer to unwind after a long day. Other nights, I'd sit outside under the stars, thinking about how far I'd come and how much further I wanted to go.

Though I was building something meaningful, a part of me couldn't shake the feeling of isolation. Calle was so close, yet so far. He rarely reached out, and I didn't have the energy to bridge the gap. It was a strange dynamic, knowing we were both carving out our own paths so close to each other yet living in entirely different worlds.

Although I had a drive and motivation to succeed, I was still depressed to the point where I found myself injecting melatonin to deal with my anxiety. The loneliness was overwhelming, even though I had ambitions larger than anything else. It was a difficult time, constantly battling the weight of isolation while striving to achieve my goals.

Björn's companionship filled some of the void, but his lifestyle was more about escapism than progress. While I appreciated his company, I knew I couldn't lose myself in that same cycle. I had a mission—to make *BestBuds* a success—and I wasn't about to let distractions pull me away.

As the weeks went by, I began brainstorming ways to take *BestBuds* to the next level. The small-town vibe of Ardala was comforting, but it wasn't the place for scaling a business. I needed to think bigger—larger markets, broader reach, and perhaps even a proper office space.

The question was: where to go from here? Would I stay in Ardala and build on the foundation I'd created, or was it time to move on again, chasing the next big opportunity? I had made plans with my Chinese partner, Phil Huang, to set-up an apartment office in Xi'An, China and had received a spreadsheet with different costs, and for 82 square meters fully furnished with TV, cellphone, etc., we would only pay 53,000 SEK a year. Great. The plan was to start up shop in China, where I could connect with so many different suppliers and start my operation internationally, using that as a base camp leaving Ardala out of the picture.

The plans for Xi'An were ambitious and enticing. An 82-square-meter fully furnished apartment for just 53,000 SEK annually seemed like a dream—complete with a TV, cellphone, and all the amenities necessary for transforming it into a base camp for *BestBuds*. China represented untapped potential: direct access to suppliers, the ability to negotiate deals in person, and the opportunity to connect with a booming market. Ardala was no longer a viable option; it was time to move forward.

But before China, there was the United Kingdom—a necessary pit stop on the road to expansion.

United Kingdom (2021 - 2022)

I arrived in the United Kingdom with a mission—to meet an upcoming partner of BestBuds who had previously provided us with some product and could potentially continue to do so. He was a fan of the movement we were building and had invited me over for dinner. His name was Matthew, and he was a very kind person. Through his connections in Italy, Spain, and Germany, he had sent deliveries of CBD-weed to me. Most of the shipments were held up at customs, except the delivery from Spain, which passed without any issues. It was of excellent quality, and I was eager to continue our relationship with Matthew.

When I arrived in the UK, I brought 11 packets of cigarettes, one more than allowed, but it turned out alright. Due to a low budget, I stayed at a hostel and met up with a Sinaloa associate who provided me with some MDMA. I ended up selling some of it as the meeting with Matthew got postponed, and I needed to book another night at the hostel.

I arrived at the restaurant a bit early and texted my mother, asking if she could send me 5 pounds so I could afford a glass of water—surprisingly, for such a fancy place, the water was free. I sat down at a table and waited for Matthew. He arrived exactly on time and detailed how he could manage the sales of our products to his clientele, expressing his admiration for our products. He also mentioned a recent sale of 100 kilograms of ISO CBD to Germany to demonstrate his capabilities. I found this promising, as I needed ISO CBD to cut my current prices—$800 per kilogram in China was my benchmark, and he could drop it to $450. We needed ISO CBD for e-liquid and our CBD Snus.

I ordered an appetiser, and Matthew assured me I could eat whatever I wanted, as he had ample funds to cover it. So, I ordered something more substantial. We had a productive and engaging meeting, solidifying our partnership. Matthew would help finalise funds for the company and assist with the sales of our products. It was a great meeting.

Afterwards, since I still had some MDMA, I asked Matthew if he wanted to purchase it, as I needed funds and wouldn't need it, given I was heading home in the coming days. He kindly refused but took me to an ATM, where he withdrew £50 and handed it to me.

After the meeting ended, I set out to find a place to stay. I booked myself into a hostel in Whitechapel for the night, knowing I'd have to figure out a way to get home the next day. My funds were gone, and the sense of victory from the meeting quickly dimmed. I reached out to Patric Ehn, who'd been supporting me and the project. When I mentioned the meeting's success, he congratulated me, but he must have sensed the shift in my mood because he asked if I was low on cash.

Patric, ever generous, offered to cover my flight home, but I felt a surge of pride or maybe guilt—I didn't want to keep taking from him. I assured him I'd manage and mentioned that I'd sell my computer and phone to make ends meet. Patric pushed back, reminding me that I'd need those tools for the work ahead, but I was too set on my plan. In my mind, it was a quick fix for a rough spot, a way to rely on myself for once, or at least that's how I justified it.

I headed to an IT shop, sold both my phone and computer, and pocketed just enough to keep myself afloat. But instead of planning my trip home, I found myself sliding back into old habits. I bought a stash of cocaine and cooked it into crack—cheap, powerful, and quick to sell. I ended up in a local club, peddling rocks to party-goers who usually sniffed their high but now faced a new temptation. Watching people fall into that spiral I knew all too well was surreal—an instant rush, followed by an insatiable craving. The regulars who tried it quickly became my best customers.

I laughed at the irony, standing in a club with pockets full of crack, with no phone, no laptop, and barely a plan for getting home.

After a few days scraping by, I stumbled upon a homeless soup kitchen in Whitechapel called "Mission"—a strange coincidence, given that it shared the name of my best friend. It was a simple setup but welcoming, and I went there for a meal, grateful for any relief from the streets.

After eating, I lingered outside, taking hits off the rocks I'd cooked. The volunteers, without judgement or hesitation, handed me a duffel bag packed with essentials: hygiene articles, a soap warmer, and even a sleeping bag. It was a small act of kindness, but it meant a lot.

That night, with my new sleeping bag in hand, I found a spot at the fire escape door outside the Royal Mail building. There was something strange and oddly peaceful about it. In that little corner, with the city sounds buzzing around me, I felt like I'd been given a small respite, however temporary.

Those mornings at Mission are still clear in my mind, especially the breakfasts—generous portions of toast piled with baked beans, crispy fries, scrambled eggs, and slices of pork. It felt like a true luxury, a meal that could easily be served at any brunch spot. Sitting there each morning, digging into that warm food, I felt like I had a bit of normalcy amid the chaos. For a moment, it didn't matter where I'd slept the night before or what I'd have to hustle for later in the day. That simple plate of food offered a brief but grounding comfort, a reminder of life's small, often overlooked pleasures.

It didn't take long for me to discover the early-morning routine at Mission. At 5 a.m., just as the doors opened, a line would form with people waiting to sign up for a hot shower and a fresh set of clothes. It reminded me of the system back at Hillerødgade 138 in Denmark—a small semblance of order in an otherwise unpredictable life.

One morning, after staying up all night smoking rocks, I finally signed up for a shower. The hot water felt like a reset, scrubbing off the grime and exhaustion of the previous day. I put on an elegant button-up shirt with dress pants they provided, and for a moment, I almost felt like myself again. That day, I picked up a brick phone at a local shop and set an alarm for 4:45 a.m., ensuring I'd be up and ready to claim a shower spot each morning. It became a ritual of sorts—a small anchor to keep me grounded, no matter what the day held ahead.

As I fell deeper into the routine, my days began to blur into each other. Funds dwindled away, and I found myself going through the motions—waiting in line for a shower at 5 a.m., getting dressed in donated clothes, eating my breakfast at Mission, and using their computer room to reconnect with the outside world. It was in one of those computer sessions that I reached out to Cortez, an old associate from my days working with the cartel. I explained my situation, hoping he might know of some opportunity to help me turn things around.

Then, one night, as I sat near my makeshift spot at the fire escape, I saw Ann-Marie again after all of those years. She seemed lost, asking where the Mission was. Playing along, I pretended not to recognize her, pointing her in the direction of the shelter but letting her know it was closed until early morning. She nodded, prepared to wait it out, and walked off.

After she left, guilt crept in, knowing she'd be spending the night on the cold pavement. I went to find her and offered her the spot next to mine, complete with cushions I'd gathered from donations. She looked at me, a mix of gratitude and weariness in her eyes, and accepted.

These days she had a brown tooth, a replacement tooth to replace one of her otherwise white ones and she explained that she had gotten raped. I felt a lot of sorrow to know that the closest I had to a mother-in-law had gotten raped and apparently gotten her tooth knocked out. I still, however, did not break character and awaited her explanation of what she did in the UK, in London of all places and why she came to seek me out. It all couldn't be a mere coincidence, did she come to pity me? To aid me? In that case, why wouldn't she simply take me to a hotel room or explain that she could help me with a flight home?

We spent the entire night talking, drifting through topics that seemed to deliberately sidestep Sweden, the past, and especially Gloria. It felt odd, as if we were strangers meeting for the first time. But I went along with it. By morning, we found ourselves at the front of the line at the shelter. I signed up for a shower, grateful for the chance, while she didn't—she probably had just come from a comfortable hotel.

Afterwards, we enjoyed a hot meal together. There was something comforting about having a familiar face around. Yet, the questions lingered, especially about the life I'd left behind. What had happened to my freshly renovated apartment in Ardala—the one with two rooms, a kitchen, and a bathroom? Did I even still have a home to return to, should the chance arise? Even if she offered to help, there was no guarantee that I'd have a place to land.

One night, as Ann-Marie and I were settled by the fire exit, passing the time with conversations that have since faded into the haze of memory, I noticed a Mexican man and an older woman across the street. Curiosity got the better of me, so I approached them. The man introduced himself as Williams, and we quickly hit it off, bonding over a shared joint. The connection was instant, like finding an unexpected ally in a foreign land.

Before long, Williams offered me a job at a Mexican kitchen he worked at, a place called Burrito Bros nestled in the nearby food court of Spitalfields. The idea of steady work—something to break the endless monotony—felt like a lifeline. The possibility of stepping into a kitchen, of working alongside him, offered a sense of normalcy amidst the chaos of my life. I took him up on the offer, feeling like perhaps, finally, I was finding a small foothold in London.

From that day forward, Williams and I would line up together every morning, waiting for our turn to shower. It became a shared routine, a small pocket of stability in a life that otherwise seemed so transient. One particular morning, as we were showering side by side, Williams caught sight of the "Aolanis" tattoo on my arm. He stared at it for a moment, his eyebrows rising in recognition, and I could see that it struck a chord.

"Aolanis... that's not a name you see every day," he remarked, tilting his head, studying the tattoo.

I nodded, bracing myself for the inevitable questions. The tattoo was more than just ink on skin—it was a link to a past that I was still carrying, a reminder of promises and oaths, of affiliations that felt miles away but still lived on under my skin.

Williams didn't press, though. He just gave a slow, understanding nod, his expression softened. "Well," he said after a pause, "it's clear we both carry a lot on our shoulders." And with that, the moment passed. But from that day on, a quiet respect settled between us—a silent acknowledgement of the pasts we each held, both invisible and indelible.

Working in the kitchen was an incredible experience—one that exceeded all my expectations. The rush of serving a large volume of customers kept me on my toes, but it was exhilarating. Our supervisor was friendly, always encouraging us, and the camaraderie between Williams and me made the shifts enjoyable. We'd joke and keep each other's spirits high, even when things got hectic. There was something so satisfying about the work, knowing we were feeding so many people and making a difference in their day.

Apart from breakfast, I now had a steady meal every day, which felt like a luxury. Not only was I taking care of myself, but I was also able to bring food to Gloria's mother. It felt good to share what I had with her, offering a small comfort amidst everything else.

One of the more unexpected twists in my journey happened when I received a tent. At first, it seemed like an odd gift, but I quickly found a practical use for it. I gave it to another homeless man, someone I'd come to know, in exchange for a favour. I asked him to store my belongings in the tent while I was away at work, and he was more than happy to oblige, especially when I offered him burritos in return. It became a simple but effective arrangement: he watched over my things during the day, and I made sure he had a decent meal. It was a small gesture of mutual support in a world where kindness often feels scarce, but it made all the difference.

As I mentioned before, I'd picked up the habit of smoking rocks. But when funds ran dry, I found myself in the company of a man named Brittish—a gentleman, in his own unusual way. Brittish was a cartel member, much like the others I'd met, but he stood out with his peculiar fetish. In exchange for the rocks he provided, he would ask me to rub his nipples. It became a strange arrangement, each of us fulfilling a need in the other, even if the circumstances were surreal.

Brittish had a certain charm to him despite this odd quirk. He'd pull up in the strangest ride I'd ever seen— one that reflected the odd personality of its owner. We'd sit together in his strange, beat-up car, passing the glass bottle back and forth. Looking back, I still wonder if it's something I should even admit to myself, let alone in a book, that I once rubbed another man's nipples in exchange for a hit.

Yet, in a strange way, Brittish and his eccentricities became just another chapter in the story of survival.

Sometimes, we smoked ice instead of crack. One of those times was a night when I retreated to the fire escape, looking for a quiet place to enjoy my buzz and let the world fade out for a while. Then, out of nowhere, Gloria appeared. I was startled, not sure if it was real or just a product of the high. But there she was, as real as anything.

In that moment, a mix of emotions surged in me. I told her that if I hadn't already smoked, I'd probably be driven to slice my throat from the anxiety. *What was really going on?* Gloria sat down next to me and, after a long silence, she told me she'd been infected with HIV. The words hung in the air, heavy and suffocating. In hindsight, I wish

I'd said, "That's okay. It just means we'll adopt babies instead." But at that moment, I didn't have those words.

Instead, as we crawled into my sleeping bag, I hugged her from behind, holding her tightly. In a shaky voice, I whispered, "Jag älskar dig"—Swedish for "I love you"—while tears streamed down my face. I cried for all the memories we'd lost, everything that had happened in our lives, and, despite everything, for the joy of seeing her again.

That very next morning, I lay wide awake, exhausted from crying the entire night. Gloria had left me with the parting words, "I'll be right back," as she went to the Mission to pick up food. I was too weak to follow her, barely able to lift my head. Ann-Marie returned with some food for me instead, her quiet support somehow comforting in the haze of my emotions. It was a surreal series of events, one after the other, each more disorienting than the last.

I still occasionally asked myself why Gloria's mother had appeared so suddenly in London, as if she were a ghost from my past. Then, one day, I found out—a revelation that struck me like a blow. One of her daughters, Nava, had been abducted, and she needed my help to get her back.

The news left me reeling. My mind spun with questions. Who could have done this? What kind of person would take a young girl from her family? As the shock settled into a cold fear, an uneasy suspicion crept in: could this have anything to do with the old drug feuds I had fought so hard to escape? The thought haunted me, casting a shadow over everything.

By that time, we had moved to a spot outside the library, on the quiet rear side of the Mission, a place where we could escape some of the city's relentless noise. Ann-Marie had become a reliable presence, often stopping by to share a smoke with me, offering me free cannabis to take the edge off. She'd be there when I wasn't at work or lost in front of the computer, her easygoing nature a steadying force in the turmoil.

Then one day, everything changed. After reaching out to a few contacts who might know something, Nava appeared—suddenly, right next to me outside the Mission. I was stunned, barely able to process the scene before me. She was thin, her frailty visible even beneath the layers of worn clothing. Her eyes, once bright, were now clouded and distant. In moments, the truth sank in: Nava was now a heroin addict. Worse yet, she had been used as a prostitute, her condition a silent testament to the horrors she'd endured.

I felt a surge of rage and helplessness. *Those bastards.* How could anyone have done this to her? The anger simmered in me, a reminder of the battles I thought I'd left behind but which now felt closer than ever.

I was set on revenge, on finding out what had happened, and simply killing everyone involved in this. Later, I passed by her in an institution where Nava was at that time. I felt relieved that the family that had broken into pieces was now put together.

Santiago Martínez was a man whose name carried whispers of fear and disgust wherever it was spoken. From the depths of Malmö's underworld to the quiet corners of Pusher Street, his reputation preceded him like a foul stench. I'd heard stories long before I crossed his path—of a man who thrived on exploiting the weak and destroying lives. Santiago wasn't just a criminal; he was a predator, an animal in the most depraved sense of the word.

He didn't merely profit from the misery of others; he revelled in it. His charm, the kind that could disarm even the most cautious, was nothing but a weapon—a polished facade to mask the rot beneath. He preyed on vulnerability, pulling people into his web and then discarding them like garbage once they'd served his purpose.

Nava was one of his many victims, but not the only one. The accounts I'd heard over time painted a picture of a man who had no moral compass, no line he wouldn't cross. He wasn't just dangerous; he was corrosive, leaving nothing but ruin in his wake.

I wasn't seeking Santiago out of blind vengeance. I was chasing justice—raw and unfiltered. A man like him didn't deserve the refuge of anonymity or the luxury of escaping the consequences of his actions. He thrived on the pain of others, and I was determined to make him feel even a fraction of what he'd inflicted.

I heard from Williams that we were "in a war." His words were heavy, loaded with a sense of urgency and camaraderie that I hadn't felt in a long time. It wasn't entirely clear who or what we were fighting against, but the way he said it made it sound like a shared battle, something larger than the chaos surrounding us.

That same day, as we sat in the dim light of our makeshift refuge, he mentioned something that caught me off guard. "You know, Hugo," he said, a faint smile tugging at his lips, "we could use you as a mascot."

"A mascot?" I echoed, unsure whether to feel flattered or offended.

"Yeah," he continued, his tone softening, "you've been through hell and back, and yet here you are, still standing. People respect that. You could inspire them, you know? Give them hope."

I wasn't entirely convinced, but there was something in his voice—an honesty, a genuine belief in what he was saying—that made me pause.

"And look," he added, leaning in slightly, "we'll help you sort yourself out. Your life, your mess. One step at a time. You don't have to do this alone."

The words hung in the air, a lifeline offered in a sea of uncertainty. For the first time in what felt like ages, I allowed myself to entertain the thought that maybe, just maybe, I could turn things around. Not overnight, not all at once, but step by step, with people like Williams by my side.

I nodded, more to myself than to him. "Alright," I said quietly, "one step at a time."

Not long after settling in, I decided to reach out to Leffe. We hadn't spoken in a while, and I was curious about how he was doing, especially after Amin's passing. To my surprise, he didn't just reply—he showed up in London, pulling up in a sleek red convertible, the engine purring like a lion. As I climbed into the passenger seat, he greeted me with a wide grin, thanking me profusely for connecting him with the cartel.

"It's all thanks to you," he said, lighting a cigarette with a gold-plated lighter. "The connections you gave me? They've opened doors I never even dreamed of."

His gratitude was genuine, and I could sense that he'd climbed the ranks. He handed me a small rock to smoke, a gesture of camaraderie, and I took it without hesitation. It was almost surreal—sitting there in a convertible with Leffe, cruising through the streets of London like nothing had ever gone wrong in our lives.

As we drove, he offered me a place to stay in the UK. "You've got potential, Hugo. Stick around here. There's room for you," he said, his tone both inviting and persuasive.

It wasn't until I started digging into what had happened to Nava that Santiago's name surfaced—a name I had heard before, whispered in the shadows of Pusher Street.

Santiago.

It was a name soaked in the grim underworld of Copenhagen's criminal networks. I hadn't thought much of it back then; it was just one of many that floated in the air, tethered to rumours of exploitation and coercion. But now, with Nava's story unfolding in jagged pieces, his name began to take on a darker weight.

"Santiago's not a street dealer," Leffe had said once, shaking his head as we shared a joint on a rainy evening. "He's the kind that doesn't get his hands dirty. He lets others do the filth for him, but you always know it's him pulling the strings."

The thought churned in my mind like a storm. There was no hard proof, no smoking gun, but instinct and whispers often carry a truth that's hard to ignore.

Nava's hollowed eyes and trembling voice were all the evidence I needed to start looking in Santiago's direction.

But I had other priorities. I wasn't ready to plant roots just yet—not in London, not anywhere. What mattered most to me at that moment was seeing that Leffe was not just surviving but thriving. Despite everything—the loss of Amin, the risks of the game—he seemed to have found his footing.

It brought me a strange sense of relief and pride. Knowing that my plans, even without my direct involvement, had somehow worked out was a bittersweet reminder that maybe I was capable of more than I gave myself credit for. For the first time in a long while, I felt a flicker of hope. After a night filled with chatter, reminiscing, and catching up with Leffe, I did something even I found surprising—I returned to my usual spot outside the library. The red convertible and the whirlwind of excitement it symbolized seemed like a fleeting escape, but the library steps felt grounding. Familiar.

There was something oddly comforting about the routine I'd built there. With a book in hand, I could slip into different worlds, letting the words carry me away from the chaos of my own life. Each story was an escape, a reminder that there were other ways to exist, other paths that people took. It was the closest thing to stability I'd had in a long time.

I spread out my blanket and leaned back, watching the city move around me. People passed by, some with curious glances, others completely oblivious. The stack of books beside me had become my shield, my escape. For a moment, it didn't matter that I was homeless, tangled in a web of dangerous connections and fleeting friendships. Here, outside the library, I found a fragile sense of calm— an anchor in the storm.

But that calm was fleeting. The weight of everything I'd been through pressed heavily on me, and soon enough, I found myself slipping into a deep emotional haze. I stayed in my sleeping bag outside the library, barely moving for nearly an entire day, cocooned beneath my blanket as if it could somehow shield me from the world.

Then, in the stillness of that despair, something unexpected happened. A girl who had walked past suddenly stopped and spun around, her hands mimicking pistols as she pointed them playfully in my direction. With a mischievous grin, she strode toward me, breaking through the heaviness like a burst of sunlight cutting through storm clouds.

"I'll be right back," she said, her tone bold and unexpected. "I'm just going to buy some booze for us." True to her word, she returned a few minutes later with a bottle of vodka and some beer. We drank together, her presence a strange but welcome distraction from my thoughts.

One thing led to another, and before I knew it, we ended up together in my sleeping bag, having sex right there on the street. Her name was Dani. It all happened so quickly. She invited me to come back to her place, but I was hesitant, wanting to stay wrapped in the familiarity of my sleeping bag. But eventually, I agreed to go with her, and as we walked, a feeling of relief settled over me. For the first time in a long time, I heard myself saying, "Now I finally feel safe."

When we arrived, we lay down together in her bed, watching Netflix. She had some weed in her drawer, and I rolled up a joint. The moment I took those first puffs, leaning out the window just as I used to in Gloria's room all those years ago, something shifted in me. It was as if I woke up, suddenly alert and questioning everything around me—unsure, at first, of what was happening or why I was there. But then, feeling the warmth of the moment, I put those thoughts aside, choosing to embrace it, hugging her close.

The next morning, Dani looked at me and, without hesitation, told me she was a sex worker.

I couldn't help but wonder—was this Cortez's doing? Was he the one magically arranging these strange "gifts" in my life? The cartel sure knew how to take care of its own, in their own twisted way. First, they'd gotten me a job. Then, a surprise visit from a girl with booze, and now a place to sleep off the streets—except it was in what I'd quickly realised was more like a brothel.

I found myself alternating between the street and Dani's place, using it as a kind of halfway refuge. But soon enough, I returned one night only to find a different girl in Dani's room. It was then I stumbled onto the truth: I was in the middle of a prostitution ring. I stayed there, caught up in a cycle of being high and lost, sleeping more than living, drifting between people who were strangers, yet somehow familiar. I ended up having a lot of sex, shameful encounters that blurred together. There were over a dozen women, some of whom I even recognized from my past, pieces of my old life resurfacing in this distorted reality.

I couldn't shake the nagging thought—was this somehow connected to my deal with the cartel? Had they opened a door here, pulling women from the ecosystem of people I'd once known? It was surreal, like a plan unfolding just beneath the surface, and yet, I was a part of it, caught in the current of something I didn't fully understand.

I still do remember that Christmas Eve—December 24th—as if it were yesterday. It was anything but traditional, yet somehow, it captured the peculiar reality of my life at the time. I found myself at what I often referred to as "the brothel," though it had originally just been *Dani's place.* The air in the small room was thick with a mix of perfume and the lingering scent of cheap wine, while the soft glow of a laptop screen cast shadows on the walls.

The room was cosy but far from luxurious. A large bed dominated the space, its unkempt sheets a testament to the constant rotation of visitors. That night, however, it was just me and a stunning blonde. She had piercing blue eyes and a laugh that could make you forget the chaos outside those walls. We weren't dressed for a fancy celebration—our version of "Christmas attire" consisted of worn-out sweatshirts and socks—but it didn't matter.

We were Netflix and chilling, as the saying goes, and for a few hours, the world outside didn't exist. The faint hum of the radiator and the occasional muffled laughter from the hall were the only reminders that we weren't alone. She curled up next to me, her head resting on my chest, as we watched some feel-good holiday movie that neither of us was really paying attention to.

The irony wasn't lost on me. While families gathered around trees adorned with ornaments and exchanged heartfelt gifts, I was here, spending Christmas Eve with a stranger in a setting that couldn't be further from home. Yet, in that moment, there was a strange sense of contentment. Maybe it was the warmth of her presence, or maybe it was the fleeting illusion of normalcy amidst the dysfunction.

It wasn't the Christmas I'd grown up with, but it was mine, and for better or worse, it was part of the story I was writing for myself.

No matter how warm and lively the times were at the brothel, the streets still called me back. My spot outside the library, oddly enough, felt like home—a patch of concrete where I found solace in the pages of books. It was a familiar rhythm: the shuffle of passing footsteps, the occasional curious glance, and the quiet hum of the city around me.

I had a vision—a bold, audacious idea that had taken root in my mind during the late hours of countless sleepless nights. I envisioned *BestBudsAB* as not just a business but a revolution in the way people thought about cannabis and, more importantly, about those the society had pushed to the margins.

The plan was simple in theory but ambitious in its scope: to give every single sex worker I encountered a steady and legitimate employment in the firm. I dreamed of building a network where those who had been dismissed and judged could find stability, dignity, and an opportunity to rebuild their lives.

This wasn't just about selling cannabis—it was about creating a family, a sanctuary. A place where the stigmatised and forgotten could reclaim their humanity. I wanted *BestBudsAB* to be more than just a name; I wanted it to be a symbol of hope and empowerment.

The challenges were clear. People would scoff at the idea, dismiss it as naive or unrealistic. But I had seen firsthand the strength and resilience of the individuals I wanted to support. They weren't weak—they were survivors, fighters. And if anyone could succeed in this endeavour, it was us, together.

The road ahead was uncertain, filled with potential pitfalls and sceptics. But as I sat down to sketch out the first steps of my plan, I felt a fire in my chest—a determination that no setback could extinguish. BestBudsAB would be more than a business; it would be a movement.

One evening, as I sat there immersed in another story, The Garden of Evening Mists by Tan Twan Eng, the flickering streetlights overhead casting a dim glow, a homeless support team approached me. Their presence, always a mixture of comfort and intrigue, carried a certain gravity. But this time, their words shattered my expectations.

"Would you like a place in a hotel for the month?"

I blinked, unsure if I had heard them correctly. Offers like this didn't just fall into one's lap. It felt almost too good to be true. For a fleeting moment, I couldn't shake the thought that this must somehow be connected to the cartel. After all, much of my life had a way of spiralling back to them in one way or another.

I didn't ask questions. The possibilities swirled in my mind, but I pushed them aside and accepted. Without hesitation, I gathered my meagre belongings and was soon standing in the lobby of a lovely hotel—a surreal upgrade from the cold concrete and thin sleeping bag that had become my home.

When I signed in, they handed me a Motorola phone. It was part of the program, a practical necessity and an unexpected gift. I turned it over in my hands, its simplicity standing in stark contrast to the complexities of my life. It was a lifeline, a tether to some semblance of stability, though now it sits forgotten in a storage unit at the psychiatric ward, a relic of that peculiar chapter in my journey.

The bed was soft, the walls were warm, and for the first time in what felt like forever, I had a door to close and a lock to turn. A fleeting moment of sanctuary in a life perpetually caught in the storm.

The hotel became my sanctuary for an entire month. Breakfast, lunch, and dinner were delivered directly to my room, complete with the polite knock of room service staff who treated me with respect and dignity. For the first time in a long while, I felt human again.

It was during this time that I met an incredible friend—a masseur who quickly became indispensable.

Not only did he take care of the chronic back pain that plagued me, but he also offered genuine camaraderie. His hands worked wonders on my aching muscles, and his conversation was just as soothing.

For that month, life felt unexpectedly luxurious, even normal. It was a stark contrast to the harshness of the streets and the unpredictability of the brothel. Yet, as much as I appreciated the comfort, I couldn't shake the feeling that this reprieve was temporary—a small oasis in a desert I wasn't ready to leave behind.

I still frequented the brothel and I had them visit me at the hotel, specifically this one lovely blond with whom I could easily share a life. I still think of her occasionally.

After the month-long stay at the first hotel, we were transported to another, equally welcoming establishment for a second month. It felt like life was giving me a second chance—a temporary escape from the chaos and uncertainty that had defined my days.

One evening, the lovely blonde from the brothel came to visit me. Her presence instantly brightened the footsteps of the hotel. I decided to share the comfort of my temporary sanctuary with her and brought out a meal for us to enjoy.

She looked at the food, smiled, and said, "I can eat it with my hands."

I couldn't help but laugh gently at her sincerity. "No, don't be silly," I replied with a grin, handing her a set of cutlery. "I've got utensils for you too."

We shared that meal in the quiet warmth of the hotel steps. It was a simple, fleeting moment, but one that left an imprint on my heart. She had an effortless way of making even the most ordinary interactions feel special.

As I write this now, I can't help but hope she stumbles upon these words one day. If she does, I hope she reaches out. Her memory lingers, a bittersweet reminder of a connection that felt genuine in a world that often felt anything but.

During my stay at the hotel, the comfort of my surroundings couldn't dull the fire burning inside me. The disrespect shown to Gloria and her family wasn't something I could let go of, and I began a process to track down the people responsible. It was a matter of principle, of honour—a line that had been crossed and needed addressing.

I reached out to Leffe, a childhood associate whose connections and instincts were sharper than ever. Over late-night calls and coded messages, we pieced together fragments of information, chasing leads until we finally landed on a name: Santiago Martínez, a Colombian.

The revelation hit me like a bad cliché. How typical and tragic—a war between Colombians and Mexicans. Two worlds clashing, a narrative as old as the trade itself. But this wasn't about drugs or territory. This was personal.

Leffe gave me the rundown: Santiago wasn't just some small-time operator. He had connections, and he wasn't someone to be underestimated. Yet, knowing this only solidified my resolve. I wasn't going into this blind. I was going to handle it carefully, methodically.

The hotel room became my war room. The Motorola phone buzzed with updates, and every lead was another piece of the puzzle. Between the plush sheets and room service meals, I prepared for a confrontation that I knew could tip the scales in unpredictable ways.

This wasn't just a fight for revenge. It was about reclaiming my name, my dignity, and, in some way, a piece of the life I had lost.

It wasn't long after I reached out to Mission on WhatsApp that he replied, his words a lifeline. He reassured me that I was welcome to stay with him for as long as I needed and, without hesitation, offered to cover my ticket back to Scandinavia. His generosity was a reminder that I wasn't entirely alone in my chaos.

The following morning, I left the comfort of the hotel behind. The luxury of daily meals, warm showers, and a soft bed had been a temporary respite, but I couldn't shake the urgency tugging at me. I boarded a flight bound for Gothenburg—my deportation from Denmark leaving me no other options.

Mission had thought ahead and arranged for my mother to meet me at the airport. Her familiar face was a strange comfort as she drove me to Malmö's train station, the city where so much of my past lingered. But in the silence of that car ride, I kept my plans and thoughts to myself. I didn't mention Gloria, Nava, or the growing fire inside me—a fire stoked by the knowledge of what Santiago Martinez had done.

The brothels, the hotels, the fleeting comforts of my recent life—they had begun to feel hollow. Even the thrill of that chaotic existence couldn't quiet the unease clawing at me. Santiago wasn't just a name or a target anymore. He was a symbol of everything wrong in the world I had been a part of for too long.

The thought of children—Nava, not even twelve— being used in such a despicable way was unbearable. It wasn't just revenge that pushed me forward now; it was a sense of justice that I couldn't ignore, no matter how tangled my own morality had become.

As the train hummed toward Copenhagen, I stared out at the passing scenery, knowing that every mile brought me closer to a confrontation I could no longer avoid.

Copenhagen

When I met Mission at Copenhagen Airport, Kastrup, it felt like a scene out of a long-lost reunion. He welcomed me with open arms, and the hug we shared was monumental—one of those embraces where words were unnecessary because everything was said through the strength of it. For a moment, the weight I had been carrying felt lighter, as though I had finally found a safe harbour amidst the chaos.

We boarded the metro together, heading toward his apartment. The hum of the train filled the silence between us, but it wasn't awkward—it was the kind of silence that speaks of familiarity and understanding.

When we arrived, Mission handed me a set of keys. "This is our place now," he said with a warmth that I hadn't felt in what seemed like forever. The gesture was simple yet profound. It wasn't just an apartment key he was handing over; it was trust, security, and the promise of a fresh start.

For the first time in a long while, I felt like I had a home—not just a roof over my head, but a place where I could breathe, reflect, and perhaps begin piecing myself back together.

I had countless unanswered questions swirling in my mind, each one heavier than the last. Yet, I remained the secretive person I'd always been, someone who kept cards close to the chest. Information, especially the kind I possessed, wasn't something I readily shared. It was power, leverage—and a liability if placed in the wrong hands. Because of this, I decided to leave Mission entirely out of what had happened—the brothel, the vendetta, and the horrors that had unfolded.

But even as I resolved to shoulder this burden alone, I was plagued with uncertainty. Where was I even supposed to start? Was I really going to hop on the next train to Skara and take matters into my own hands? The image of Santiago's throat slashed open flitted through my mind. It was graphic, visceral, but disturbingly clear.

Sure, that was an option. It seemed plausible.

Then another thought crept in—what about a gunshot to the back of his head? It felt cleaner, more efficient, but no less final. Leffe's connections came to mind. If he could get me hand grenades when I was just 17, surely securing a handgun now, at 22, would be child's play. The idea lingered, tantalizingly simple.

Still, there was an unease in my chest, a gnawing sensation that wouldn't let up. This wasn't just a question of logistics; it was a question of morality, of consequences. Revenge was a seductive mistress, promising closure and satisfaction, but I wasn't naïve enough to believe it would be that simple. Was this really the path I wanted to take? Or was I just spiralling further into a darkness I might never escape?

As I sat there with these thoughts consuming me, the weight of the decisions I had yet to make felt suffocating. Every scenario played out in my mind, but none of them led to peace. Just more chaos, more blood, and a version of myself I wasn't sure I wanted to meet.

I spent the next few days pacing around Mission's apartment, my mind a battlefield of rage and doubt. The city hummed with its usual indifference, but I couldn't bring myself to engage with it. The metro rattled past outside the window like a metronome, counting down the seconds until I needed to act—or abandon the thought entirely.

Mission, kind as always, noticed my distracted state. He tried to check in, to pull me out of whatever darkness he thought I was sinking into, but I deflected his concern. He didn't need to know what was going on in my mind.

He wouldn't understand, and even if he did, he'd only try to stop me.

Late one evening, I found myself scrolling through old contacts, piecing together fragments of information. Santiago wasn't the kind of man who disappeared easily. People like him left traces—whispers in bars, glimpses in alleys. I reached out to Leffe, not for a gun or any elaborate plan, but for his connections.

"Leffe," I said when he picked up.

"Well, if it isn't Hugo," he replied, his voice carrying a mix of surprise and suspicion. "What do you need?"

"I need to find someone," I said.

There was a pause. "What kind of someone?"

"Santiago. You know the name?"

Leffe exhaled sharply. "Yeah, I've heard of him. What's your business with him?"

"That's my business," I said, keeping my tone flat. Leffe didn't push, but I could sense his curiosity. Instead, he told me to give him a day or two.

True to his word, Leffe called me back the next evening with a location. Santiago was staying in a rundown apartment complex in Skara, a place that barely deserved to be called a home.

"Be careful," Leffe said before hanging up.

I didn't respond. Care wasn't part of the plan. On my way to Skara, I stopped in Malmö to meet Leffe. He was waiting in his usual spot, leaning against his car, a cigarette dangling between his fingers. He didn't waste time on small talk.

"You're serious about this?" he asked, his eyes searching mine.

I nodded. Leffe opened the car's trunk and pulled out a small handgun. He handed it to me, his expression grim. "If you're going to do this, you need to be prepared. Don't hesitate, Hugo."

The weight of the gun was surprising, heavier than I'd expected. I tucked it into my bag, feeling its presence like a brand against my side. Leffe placed a hand on my shoulder before I left. "Don't let this consume you," he said, his tone uncharacteristically soft.

I didn't respond. I wasn't sure if I could make that promise.

When Santiago's name resurfaced in the context of Nava, it clicked like a missing piece in an ugly puzzle. His history, his dealings, the company he kept—it all pointed in the same grim direction. Santiago wasn't just another player; he was a parasite feeding off the vulnerable, a spectre that had haunted more than just one innocent life.

Skara

The train ride to Skara was quiet, the hum of the wheels on the tracks the only sound accompanying my thoughts. I replayed everything I knew about Santiago, every piece of information that had brought me to this moment. By the time I arrived, I felt like I was moving on autopilot.

The apartment complex was as grim as I'd imagined—peeling paint, broken windows, the faint stench of mildew. I found his door on the second floor, my steps careful and deliberate.

I didn't knock. I didn't hesitate. I pushed the door open and stepped inside, my heart pounding like a war drum. Santiago was there, seated at a rickety table, his back to me.

The weight of the gun pressed against my side as I slowly drew it from my underwear. Its cold steel felt heavy in my hand, a stark contrast to the fire coursing through my veins. I raised it, aiming directly at him.

When he turned, his expression shifted from confusion to recognition to something darker. "Hugo," he said, his voice low and steady.

"Santiago," I replied, my voice equally calm, though inside I was anything but.

The room felt like it was holding its breath, the silence heavy and suffocating. Everything I had carried with me—rage, grief, determination—boiled over in that moment.

"You know why I'm here," I said, taking a step closer, the barrel unwavering.

He didn't answer at first, his wide eyes darting between the gun and my face. Then he raised his hands slowly, palms out. "Hugo, let's talk—"

"Shut up," I snapped, my finger tightening ever so slightly on the trigger. "You've had your chance to talk."

Santiago shifted in his chair, his movements slow and deliberate. "Listen, I didn't—"

"Don't you dare lie to me," I interrupted, my voice cold as ice. "You think I don't know what you've done? You think you can just walk away from everything like it never happened?"

I moved closer, the gun now just inches from his face. The sight of his fear should have been satisfying, but it wasn't. It only made the storm inside me rage harder.

His chair creaked as he leaned back slightly, his hands trembling. "Hugo, please. You don't want to do this."

For a brief moment, the tension between us felt unbearable. Then, in an act of desperation, Santiago lunged forward, his hands swiping at the gun.

Instinctively, I stepped back and struck him across the temple with the butt of the weapon. He crumpled to the floor, dazed and groaning. Without thinking, I grabbed a belt lying nearby and tied his hands tightly behind his back.

I shoved him back into the chair, his head slumped forward. His wide eyes darted around the room, looking for an escape that didn't exist.

"You're not going anywhere," I said, my voice low and steady, though my insides churned. The gun remained in my hand, its presence a constant reminder of the choice I'd yet to make.

The air in the room felt stifling, the weight of what I'd just done—and what I was about to do—pressing down on me like a lead blanket. Santiago was at my mercy, and for the first time, I realized just how far I was willing to go.

Instead of killing him outright, I stayed. For the next two weeks, Santiago and I shared the apartment, though "shared" is hardly the right word. He was a prisoner in his own home, and I was his captor.

He cooked meals in silence, his hands trembling as he chopped vegetables or stirred a pot. I allowed him just enough freedom to move around the apartment but kept him under constant watch. The fear in his eyes was intoxicating, a reminder of the power I held.

As the days blurred together in the dingy apartment, I started noticing little things about Santiago that didn't quite add up. He had always been a sly operator, but something about his behaviour struck me as calculated in ways I hadn't fully understood before. It wasn't until I found a stack of paperwork on his cluttered kitchen table that the pieces began to fall into place.

The documents were official—forms stamped with seals from government agencies, filled out in painstaking detail. At first glance, they seemed unremarkable. But as I read further, it became clear what Santiago had been up to. He had been claiming disability benefits for years, all based on the fabricated claim that he had a severe mental impairment.

I stared at the forms, the words blurring together as my anger simmered just below the surface. The irony wasn't lost on me—this man, who had caused unimaginable suffering, was playing society like a fiddle, milking it for every euro he could.

I confronted him later that evening, holding the forms out like evidence in a trial. "So, this is your game now? Pretending to be someone you're not to scam the system?"

His face twisted into a smirk, an infuriating mix of arrogance and amusement. "It's not a crime to survive, Hugo," he said, leaning back in his chair as if my discovery meant nothing. "You should know that better than anyone."

The audacity of his response hit me like a slap. He spoke as though his deceit was a badge of honour, a testament to his cunning. But all I could see was a man willing to manipulate anyone and anything, without remorse, to serve his own interests.

At night, I barely slept, my thoughts a tangled web of anger, regret, and hesitation. Santiago, on the other hand, slept fitfully, if at all. I could hear him tossing and turning in the next room, the faint creak of the bedframe a soundtrack to his torment.

Occasionally, he tried to reason with me, his voice shaky as he begged for mercy. "Hugo, please, you don't have to do this. Let me go. I'll disappear. You'll never see me again."

His words only deepened my resolve. He had taken something from me—something that could never be replaced. He needed to feel the weight of his actions, to understand the consequences.

It was late afternoon when Johan showed up at Santiago's apartment. I wasn't expecting anyone, and the sudden knock on the door set my nerves on edge. Santiago, still untied but weakened, looked toward the door, his eyes flickering with a hint of hope.

I hesitated for a moment, then quietly approached, slipping the knife into the waistband of my jeans. When I opened the door, Johan was standing there, a mixture of concern and confusion on his face.

"Hugo?" he said, his voice filled with surprise. "What are you doing here? I came to check on Santiago. He's been ignoring my calls."

I had known Johan by selling hash to him earlier in my life.

I stepped back to let him in. "Come in," I replied, keeping my voice calm despite the tension inside me.

Johan entered, glancing around the dimly lit apartment before his eyes landed on Santiago. He stood in the doorway, his posture stiff and uncertain. Santiago was standing too, just a few steps away in the hallway, his body language pleading for help but trapped in a delicate situation. He made a few slow movements but didn't speak.

"What's going on, Hugo?" Johan demanded, his voice rising. "What have you done to him?"

I locked the door behind him, and with a quiet step forward, I calmly said, "It's not what it looks like. It's between me and Santiago. You need to leave, Johan."

Johan took a step toward Santiago, his concern growing, but I could see the hesitation in his eyes. He knew something wasn't right but wasn't sure what to make of it.

"I don't think you understand," I said, my voice still steady but with an underlying edge. "I need you to leave. Now."

Johan's gaze shifted from me to Santiago, and for a moment, I saw the confusion and fear in his eyes. He wasn't sure what to do, but I saw the determination in his posture; he wasn't going to back down easily.

"Why are you doing this, Hugo? This isn't you!" he said, his voice strained.

I took a deep breath, pulling the knife from my waistband, and in one smooth motion, I levelled it with his chest, the blade catching the light just enough to send a chill down his spine. "I said, leave," I repeated, my voice unwavering.

Johan's face went pale as he instinctively took a step back, his eyes never leaving the knife. "Please, Hugo," he said, desperation creeping into his voice. "You don't have to do this. We can talk this out, okay? Just let Santiago go."

I shook my head slowly, my grip tightening around the knife. "It's too late for that."

Santiago, sensing the danger, tensed up, but Johan continued to try and reason with me. "This isn't the way, Hugo! You're better than this!"

But I didn't care. I wasn't going to back down. I needed him out of the apartment. I needed to deal with Santiago.

Finally, Johan raised his hands in surrender, his eyes scanning the door. "Fine, I'll go. But this isn't over. I won't let you do this."

I nodded once, keeping the knife steady in my hand as he made his way to the door. As he left, I didn't look away. I wasn't done yet. Santiago had been nothing but a piece in this game, and I wasn't about to let him slip away so easily.

The door clicked shut behind Johan, and the silence that followed felt deafening. My eyes went back to Santiago, who was visibly shaken but still standing in the same spot, as if unsure of his next move.

"You're not going anywhere," I muttered.

On the fourteenth night, I reached my breaking point. The suffocating atmosphere of the apartment, the constant presence of Santiago, the memories of Nava—it all became too much.

I decided it was time to end it. The thought had festered long enough, and the weight of indecision was eating me alive. But as I glanced at the clock, seeing the dim digits flash *5:00 a.m.*. Shooting him would be too noisy, far too likely to wake the neighbours. No, if this was going to happen, it had to be quiet. Calculated.

I set the table for two, laying out plates of tacos with a precision that felt almost ceremonial. Santiago watched me warily, his movements slow as he took his seat. The fear in his eyes had grown dull, as if he had resigned himself to whatever fate awaited him.

"Eat," I said simply, sitting down across from him.

He hesitated but eventually picked up a taco. His hands trembled as he brought it to his mouth, taking small, cautious bites.

"You know why we're here," I said, my voice devoid of emotion.

Santiago froze, the taco slipping from his fingers and landing on the plate with a soft thud. "Hugo, please—"

But his plea fell on deaf ears. I reached for the knife I had placed beside my plate. In one swift motion, I plunged it into his throat. The blade sank in easily, and his eyes widened in shock. He made a gurgling sound, blood spilling from the wound and pooling on the table.

I didn't stop there. Two more strikes followed, each one more visceral than the last.

When it was over, I sat back, staring at the lifeless body slumped in the chair. The room was silent, save for the sound of blood dripping onto the floor.

When it was over, I sat there in the silence, the knife still in his throat. The weight of what I had done settled over me like a suffocating blanket, but I knew there was no turning back. Santiago was gone, and with him, a part of myself I would never get back.

I yanked the knife out of his throat with a sickening squelch, blood spraying across the kitchen table and floor. His body slumped lifelessly in the chair, and for a moment, I just stood there, staring at the mess I had created. The room reeked of iron and finality.

Without thinking, I drove the blade back into his neck twice more, the motions excessive but strangely cathartic. The knife, dripping with his blood, was now a symbol of the line I had crossed. I walked over to the dishwasher, pulled it open, and dropped the blade inside. I ran some water over my hands and closed it, as if washing a plate after dinner.

The reality of what I had done hit me in flashes, like a strobe light in my mind. I couldn't stay in the bloodied clothes. I made my way to the bathroom, peeling off the soaked fabric and tossing it into the washing machine. I poured in an excessive amount of detergent, set the cycle, and let the machine whir to life.

Under the harsh fluorescent lights of the bathroom, I stepped into the shower, letting the water run hot. I scrubbed at my skin furiously, every motion mechanical, as if I could erase the memory of his blood along with the stains. The water swirling down the drain turned from red to pink to clear, and yet I kept scrubbing, as though the act could absolve me.

When I finally stepped out, my skin was raw from the friction. I wrapped a towel around my waist and ventured into his bedroom. The room was a mess, much like the rest of his place—clothes strewn about, an unmade bed, a faint smell of cigarettes and cheap cologne lingering in the air. I rifled through his wardrobe, searching for something clean, something that didn't reek of him.

Eventually, I found a pair of jeans and a Hawaiian-looking T-shirt. They fit well enough. As I pulled the shirt over my head, I caught a glimpse of myself in the cracked mirror hanging on the wall. My face was pale, my eyes hollow. The person staring back at me felt like a stranger—a reflection of a man who had just taken a life and was now trying to piece himself back together in the aftermath.

Dressed and composed, I left the bedroom.

After tidying up Santiago's apartment to the best of my ability, I felt an overwhelming need to clear my head. The heaviness in my chest was suffocating, and I needed an outlet. I grabbed my gym bag, one of the few things I always made sure to have ready, and headed out to a nearby gym I'd scoped out earlier.

The gym was mostly empty, the rhythmic clang of weights and the soft hum of treadmills the only sounds filling the space. I slipped on a pair of gloves and started with the bench press, focusing on the weight and my breathing. With every rep, I tried to push out the thoughts swirling in my mind. The act of working out felt grounding, like I was reclaiming a small piece of control in a world that had spiralled so far out of hand.

Next came the punching bag. I threw myself into it, each punch harder than the last, my knuckles stinging through the gloves. The image of Santiago flashed in my mind, but I didn't let myself linger on it. The punching bag became my release, a way to channel the tension coursing through my body.

When I finally finished, drenched in sweat and slightly calmer, I checked my phone. Patric had texted back, confirming he could meet me at a cafe nearby. He always had a way of coming through when I needed him, no questions asked.

I made my way to the cafe, my gym bag slung over my shoulder. Patric was already seated at a table, sipping on a cup of coffee. His face lit up when he saw me, and he waved me over.

"Hey, you look like you've been through a war," he joked, gesturing at my dishevelled appearance.

I gave him a tired smile and sat down. We exchanged pleasantries for a bit before I got to the point. "Patric, I need some cash for a train ticket back to Copenhagen," I said, trying to keep my voice steady.

He nodded without hesitation. "Of course, man. Here," he said, pulling out his wallet and handing me a few crisp bills.

"Thanks, Patric. I'll pay you back soon," I said, pocketing the money.

"Don't worry about it," he replied with a shrug. "Just make sure you're okay."

We talked for a little while longer, but my mind was already preoccupied with the pressing need to return to Copenhagen. The conversation with Patric felt distant, like white noise behind the chaos swirling in my thoughts. After thanking him for his help and saying our goodbyes, I headed straight toward the train station, the cash for my ticket burning in my pocket.

On the way, I made a deliberate stop at a nearby dumpster. The gun, still heavy with the weight of unfulfilled purpose, rested in my bag. I pulled it out cautiously, ensuring no one was around, and began wiping it down meticulously with the inside of my shirt. Every surface, every crevice—it had to be spotless. The last thing

I needed was to leave behind any trace that could link me to the weapon. Once I was satisfied, I wrapped it in a plastic bag I had found picked up in Santiago's apartment and dropped it into the dumpster. The sound of it hitting the metal echoed faintly, a small yet significant weight lifted from my shoulders. I stood there for a moment, staring into the dark void of the dumpster, before turning away. I adjusted my bag on my shoulder and walked briskly to the station. Each step took me closer to Copenhagen, but also further from the storm I had left behind. Or so I thought.

As I stood at the train station in Skara, the weight of what had transpired over the last two weeks pressed down on me. The memories of Santiago's fear-stricken face, the moments of hesitation, and the final act of violence played in my mind like a loop I couldn't escape. I told myself it was justice, but doubt clawed at the edges of my resolve.

The platform was quiet, and I boarded the train, sinking into a window seat as the engine roared to life.

On the train back to Copenhagen, I tried to focus on the fleeting scenery outside the window, but it felt like a mirage—a world I no longer belonged to. Every whistle of the train seemed to echo a question I wasn't ready to answer: What would happen if this all caught up to me? My hands gripped the seat's edges, not out of fear of the train's speed, but the velocity at which my actions were unravelling my life.

When the train finally pulled into Copenhagen Central Station, I stepped off with a mix of relief and apprehension. The familiar sights and sounds of the city welcomed me back, but I knew I wasn't returning as the same person who had left.

Copenhagen

When I arrived back at the apartment, exhaustion hit me like a wave. The past two weeks had been a blur of chaos and sleepless nights, and I barely managed to drag myself through the door before collapsing onto the king-size bed that I shared with Mission. The mattress felt like a cloud after everything I had been through, and I let myself sink into it, hoping for just an hour of peace.

I must have barely closed my eyes when the sound of drilling snapped me awake. Mission was in the room, unpacking a brand-new smart TV and mounting it on the wall. His energy was contagious, his enthusiasm lighting up the room despite my groggy state.

"Hey, sorry to wake you," he said with a grin as he adjusted the mounting brackets. "But you're gonna love this. I finally got us a proper setup." I gave him a sleepy thumbs-up, muttering something incoherent before burying my face in the pillow. Mission always had a way of keeping the atmosphere light, and I was grateful for it, even if I was too drained to show it.

As he wrapped up the installation, he casually mentioned, "By the way, I invited a couple of the guys over tonight. Figured we could use some drinks and a good time."

I nodded, too tired to argue. A few drinks sounded like exactly what I needed to distract myself from the whirlwind of the past fortnight. I got up, took a quick shower to shake off the grogginess, and joined Mission in the living room as he set up snacks and drinks.

That evening, the apartment came alive. The two friends Mission had invited were in high spirits, their laughter filling the space as we clinked glasses and shared stories. The music was loud, the drinks were flowing, and for a few hours, it felt like everything was back to normal. Ironically, one of the friends Mission had invited was Columbian. The irony wasn't lost on me, but I kept my composure, laughing along with everyone else. I hadn't mentioned a word to Mission about what had happened in Skara. Not because I didn't trust him, but because I didn't want to pull him into the darkness that still lingered over me.

As the night wore on, the alcohol dulled the edges of my thoughts, and for a brief moment, I let myself believe that things could be as simple as they were in that room— a group of friends, good drinks, and laughter. But deep down, I knew the weight of what had happened would catch up with me eventually. For now, though, I was content to let the night carry me away.

The time when everything caught up with me came sooner than expected—less than a day later. Mission and I were still half-asleep, tangled in the comfort of the king-size bed, when his phone blared loudly, jolting us both awake. He groaned, reaching over to pick it up, and glanced at the screen.

"It's your mom," he mumbled, still groggy.

My heart immediately started pounding. I motioned for him to put it on speaker, my gut already bracing for something bad.

As soon as the line connected, my mother's voice came through, trembling and frantic. "Mission, have you seen Ernst? Twelve policemen—armed with heavy artillery—stormed my house this morning. They lined me and your brother against the wall, shouting, demanding to know where he is!"

Mission's eyes widened as he looked at me for answers. I froze, panic flooding through me. I quickly placed a finger over my lips, signalling for him to stay quiet about my presence. My mother continued, her voice thick with fear.

"They're saying he's involved in something serious," she continued, "and they're desperate to find him. Please, Mission, if you've seen him, tell me."

Mission stumbled through the conversation, playing dumb. "No, I haven't seen him lately," he lied, his tone uneasy.

The call ended, but the air between us remained heavy. Mission turned to me immediately, his face a mix of confusion and concern. "What the hell was that about?" he asked, his voice low but sharp.

I felt the weight of my actions bearing down on me. For the first time in our years of friendship, I lied to him. "Probably something to do with money laundering," I muttered, trying to sound nonchalant but failing miserably.

Mission didn't press further, but the look in his eyes said it all—he didn't believe me, and he knew there was more to the story. The trust between us, so steadfast until now, was strained in an instant.

I slumped back onto the bed, staring at the ceiling as the reality of the situation sank in. My mother and brother had been dragged into the chaos I had created, and now it wasn't just me on the run. The lines between my criminal life and the people I cared about were blurring, and there was no easy way to separate them.

Mission sat silently beside me, gripping his phone tightly as if expecting it to ring again at any moment. The tension in the room was suffocating, with unspoken questions hanging in the air between us. Mission's loyalty was unwavering, but I knew he was worried. He didn't press for details, and I didn't offer any. For now, all that mattered was figuring out my next move—and fast.

Seeking advice, I called my father. I carefully navigated the conversation, omitting the grittier details, and explained the situation as vaguely as possible. His response was simple: "Go to the police station in Malmö and sort it out." His confidence struck a chord in me, and for a brief moment, I believed it could be that easy.

Deep down, I reassured myself that there was no solid proof tying me to Santiago's death. I had cleaned up meticulously—washing my bloody clothes, scrubbing surfaces for fingerprints, and even placing the knife in the dishwasher. These were precautions I couldn't explain to my father, but they bolstered my belief that I could beat the case.

As the call ended, I felt a flicker of resolve. Despite the risks, I began crafting a plan. What I didn't know was whether my confidence would lead to redemption or my ultimate undoing.

After the lively celebration we held on the 25th, I took some time to unwind and gather my thoughts. However, the calm didn't last long. On the 26th, Mission received another call from my mother. Her voice carried the same mix of frustration and fear as before.

She explained that the police had shown up at her house again, this time more aggressive than ever. They had pushed her and my brother up against the walls as they searched for me, their weapons drawn and their tone unyielding. It was clear they weren't going to back down, and my family was paying the price for my actions.

Realizing I couldn't keep dragging them into this ordeal, I decided to face it head-on. Early on the morning of the 27th, I packed my things and left for Malmö. The weight of the situation was heavy on my shoulders, but I knew it was time to confront whatever awaited me. There was no running from it anymore.

Custody

I arrived at the police station in Malmö on the 27th of May 2022, and upon introducing myself, I was immediately detained on suspicion of having murdered Santiago Martínez.

As they began a frisk search, one of the officers, a strikingly handsome woman with sharp features and an air of authority, asked, "Do you have anything sharp in your pockets?"

"I've got a pen in my left jeans pocket," I replied calmly.

The male officer, who had a nerdy appearance with thick-rimmed glasses and an awkward posture, quickly retrieved the pen and gave a slight nod to his colleague. Their contrasting energies—her commanding and composed, his meticulous and cautious—made the situation feel even more surreal.

After the frisk search, I was led to a holding cell. The sound of the heavy metal door clanging shut echoed ominously in the empty hallway. The cell was cold and sterile, with nothing but a hard bench and a stainless-steel toilet in the corner. I sat down, leaning my head against the wall, and stared at the ceiling, trying to process the gravity of what was happening.

The door opened a short while later, and the two officers reappeared.

"Follow us," the woman said, her tone neutral but firm.

They escorted me down a dimly lit corridor to an interrogation room. Inside, a plain table and two chairs awaited. The fluorescent lights buzzed softly, adding to the oppressive atmosphere.

Once seated, I was faced with another officer—this one was middle-aged, with a calm but calculating demeanor. He introduced himself as Inspector Hansson.

"We're going to ask you some questions about Santiago Martínez," Hansson began, his voice steady but probing. "This is your chance to explain your version of what happened on the night of May 25th. You have the right to remain silent, but anything you say may be used in court."

I nodded, my mind racing.

"Where were you that night?" Hansson asked, leaning slightly forward.

"I was sleeping," I replied without hesitation. "On Santiago's couch."

The female officer, who stood by the door with her arms crossed, raised an eyebrow but didn't interrupt.

Hansson tilted his head slightly, scrutinizing me. "So, you stayed overnight at his place?"

"Yeah," I said. "I was crashing there for the night. I fell asleep on the couch, woke up the next morning, and left. That's all."

The nerdy officer jotted something down in his notebook, his pen scratching loudly against the paper.

"And what was your relationship with Santiago?" Hansson pressed.

"We were acquaintances," I said carefully. "Not close or anything, but we knew each other."

The questions kept coming, each one chipping away at my resolve. They wanted to know why I was there, what time I had arrived, and if anyone could verify my story. I stuck to my fabricated alibi, insisting that I had simply been sleeping on Santiago's couch and knew nothing about what had happened to him.

The woman officer occasionally glanced at me, her piercing gaze making me feel as though she could see through my lies. The male officer, meanwhile, focused on his notes, nodding occasionally but avoiding direct eye contact.

After what felt like hours, the interrogation ended. I was led back to the holding cell, the door clanging shut behind me once again. I sat down on the cold bench, my mind replaying the conversation over and over. Did they believe me? Could they poke holes in my story?

The uncertainty gnawed at me, but I knew one thing: I had to stick to my story, no matter what.

After a long day of interrogation, I was informed that I would be transported to Helsingborg to spend the night. The officers escorted me to the transport van, where the atmosphere was cold and quiet, the hum of the engine the only sound as we drove through the night.

When I arrived at the detention facility in Helsingborg, they handed me a portable DVD player along with a season of *Solsidan*. It felt surreal—here I was, detained under serious accusations, yet being given a piece of Swedish comedy to pass the time. I settled into the dimly lit cell, the hum of the DVD player a strange comfort against the sterile environment. Watching the lighthearted antics of *Solsidan* was oddly grounding, even if the laughter felt hollow in my current predicament.

The next morning, my brief stay in Helsingborg came to an end. The guards loaded me into another transport van. This time, the destination was Mariestad. The journey was long, the roads winding through the Swedish countryside as the weight of what lay ahead pressed heavily on my chest. Each kilometre brought me closer to an uncertain future.

I couldn't help but think about the absurdity of it all—the twists and turns of my life leading up to this point. As the van rolled into Mariestad, I braced myself for what was to come.

Mariestad

Custody in Mariestad was, in many ways, a strange mix of routine and limbo—a world removed from the chaos that had led me there. The facility itself was surprisingly accommodating for what it was. There was a kitchen available where we could bake things if we wanted, which felt almost surreal given the circumstances. I remember the smell of freshly baked goods wafting through the air, a stark contrast to the sterile and controlled environment around me.

There was also a room where I could watch movies, offering a brief escape into other worlds. It became a ritual of sorts for me—an hour or two spent losing myself in stories far removed from my reality. Then there was the yard, a small outdoor space where we could go to smoke cigarettes. It wasn't much, just a patch of concrete enclosed by high walls, but it was a reminder of the outside world, of freedom.

A highlight of my time in custody was my lawyer. She was fantastic—sharp, articulate, and determined. She visited me regularly, bringing not just legal advice but a sense of reassurance that I desperately needed. I had made the choice early on to deny all accusations. I told her that I had simply slept over at Santiago's place, crashed on the couch, and gone to the gym with him the next morning. I constructed a narrative that was easy to believe and stuck to it like glue.

The truth, of course, was far more complicated. But I lied to my lawyer. Even though she was there to defend me, I couldn't bring myself to tell her what had really happened. I justified it as self-preservation, but deep down, I knew it was more than that. Admitting the truth felt like admitting defeat, and I wasn't ready for that—not yet.

Each day in Mariestad, custody felt like a balancing act between the persona I presented and the turmoil I kept buried. The routines, the lawyer's visits, the cigarettes in the yard—they were all small distractions from the weight of what lay ahead.

In Mariestad, I had found myself a routine of always going to wash my face every morning using a face-wash bought in the kiosk. You know, the "kiosk" sheet of paper that we receive once a week and fill in what we want to buy from the 100 crowns sum that we receive. Since my cell was seated on the opposite side of a toilet without a mirror, so every morning, I had to go all the way across the corridor to reach a toilet with a mirror.

In Mariestad, I found myself clinging to small routines to maintain a sense of normalcy. Every morning, without fail, I'd grab my face wash—a small luxury purchased from the kiosk sheet we were given weekly. The 100 crowns we received were barely enough for extras, but that face wash became a crucial part of my day. My cell was across from a toilet, but it didn't have a mirror. So, I'd walk down the corridor to a bathroom with one, making it a ritual that anchored me in the chaos.

One morning, however, everything unravelled. As I prepared to head to the mirror-equipped bathroom, the warden stopped me.

"You're not allowed to go there," he said firmly.

"Yes, I am. I do this every morning," I replied, already feeling irritation bubbling beneath the surface.

"No, you're not allowed," he reiterated, his tone leaving no room for argument.

That was the tipping point. "YES, I a.m. GOING," I snapped, pushing past him in defiance.

What happened next escalated faster than I could have anticipated. He stepped into my path, trying to block me, and instinctively, my frustration exploded into physicality. A brief struggle followed, and before I knew it, I landed a punch squarely in his eye socket.

All of it—over something as trivial as my morning face-wash routine. The absurdity of it hit me later, but in that moment, it felt like defending the last shred of control I had in a world where so little was mine to dictate.

Due to this my transportation was scheduled to get to Gothenburg. I was going to a maximum security holding cell.

Gothenburg

In Gothenburg, I settled into the routine of confinement with a grim determination. The atmosphere was oppressive, the weight of my charges lingering in every interaction with the guards and every step I took within the high-security walls. I was labelled a high-risk inmate—not just because of the murder charge but also due to the incident in Mariestad, where I had lashed out violently over what now seemed like a trivial argument about face-washing.

Every move I made was under scrutiny. My cell was stripped of anything unnecessary, leaving only the bare essentials. Meals were delivered with the kind of cautiousness one might reserve for a caged predator. I was aware of the reputation preceding me, and I knew it was one more hurdle I'd need to navigate carefully.

At first, the police interrogations felt almost routine. I stuck to my story, denying involvement in Santiago Martínez's murder and weaving a narrative that kept me at arm's length from any direct evidence. My strategy was simple: answer what I couldn't avoid, sidestep what I could, and never, under any circumstances, offer them anything more than what they already knew.

For four months, this strategy worked. The investigators grew visibly frustrated, their attempts to rattle me bouncing off the armour of composure I had built around myself. Each session felt like a chess match, with both sides trying to outwit the other.

Then, it happened. One afternoon, the lead investigator entered the room with a confidence I hadn't seen before. He carried a folder, and the way he set it on the table told me it contained something significant.

"Let's see if this jogs your memory," he said, opening the folder to reveal photographs of my bloody clothes.

For a split second, I felt my composure falter. The images were undeniable proof, stark against the pale backdrop of the interrogation room. I had been meticulous—washing my clothes, wiping down fingerprints, and placing the knife in Santiago's dishwasher. But now, it was clear: the washing machine hadn't run.

The investigator explained it to me, almost mockingly. "The machine got stuck," he said, "caught between two different programs. It never started."

The weight of his words was crushing. I had assumed my tracks were covered, that my calculated cleanup had eliminated any evidence. Yet, something as trivial as a technical glitch had unravelled the illusion of my careful planning. I knew my approach had to change. If I continued as I was, I risked slipping up, giving them a thread to pull. Instead, I pivoted. The moment they presented the photos, I leaned into a new narrative: insanity.

At first, it was subtle—slightly erratic behaviour during questioning, a distant stare, muttered responses that seemed to trail off into unrelated thoughts. The goal was to plant seeds of doubt about my mental state.

As the days went on, I escalated my act. I began twitching during interrogations, muttering incoherent phrases, and refusing to make eye contact. Sometimes, I would laugh at nothing or cry without warning. My answers became more fragmented, like pieces of a puzzle that didn't fit together. The investigators were thrown off balance. They didn't know whether I was genuinely losing touch with reality or if this was a calculated performance. Some of them tried to provoke me, raising their voices and demanding clarity. Others shifted to a softer tone, speaking to me as if I were a fragile child.

But I gave them nothing concrete. My act was convincing enough to cast doubt, and that doubt was my lifeline. If they couldn't trust my state of mind, their case would lose its foundation.

The frustration in the room was palpable. The lead investigator, once confident, now seemed unsure of how to proceed. Their carefully crafted strategy had hit an unexpected roadblock, and I could see them grappling with how to navigate it. Back in my cell, I replayed each interrogation in my mind, analyzing every question, every response. I knew the act had to be flawless—any slip could undo everything I'd worked toward.

The waiting became its own form of torment. Days stretched into weeks, the monotony broken only by the sound of footsteps in the corridor or the occasional clatter of metal trays. But I clung to my new strategy, knowing it was my best chance of avoiding a lengthy prison sentence.

As the months passed, I began to notice a change in the way the guards treated me. Their watchful eyes seemed to hold a mix of pity and caution, as if they were unsure whether I was a threat or a victim of my own mind.

It wasn't freedom, but it was a step closer to the outcome I needed. Now, it was a matter of endurance—waiting out the system and ensuring my act held up long enough to get me to the psychiatric ward instead of a prison cell.

I spent most of my time in the holding cell conducting "business plans" to keep my mind sharp and alert — anything to keep my mind occupied. I will write about them now in this book.

Business Plans

All of my business plans were meticulously crafted on physical paper during the 11-month period I was detained. Some plans were scribbled on squared math paper, while others were on lined paper. These documents represent the culmination of countless hours of thought and planning. They are a testament to my determination to create a future beyond the walls of my cell.

These papers are now stored inside my storage unit in the psychiatric ward. Scans of these documents will be taken and uploaded to my website, HatakeHugo.com. This collection of plans includes various business ideas, strategies, and proposals that I hope to bring to fruition once I regain my freedom. My time in custody has not been idle; it has been a period of intense introspection and planning for a better future.

Amongst the first things that I did on paper was to create a quote on quote programming language - something that I could utilise in order to rapidly design business plans.

ChinaTown/CT

Overview:

The ChinaTown (CT) initiative aims to address housing shortages in rural areas by mass-producing modular building components. These components, akin to Lego pieces, will facilitate the rapid construction of houses and towns, providing affordable and efficient housing solutions. All of the CTs are to include thermal enhancing climate-friendly curtains manufactured by **ClimateCurtainsAB**.

Key Components:

1. Modular Building System:

- Development and production of modular building pieces/bricks.
- These pieces will be designed to fit together seamlessly, allowing for the quick assembly of various types of structures.
- Focus on sustainability and durability in the design and materials used.

2. Mass Production and Deployment:

- Establishment of production facilities to manufacture the modular pieces on a large scale.

- Implementation of logistics and supply chain strategies to deliver these pieces to rural areas efficiently.
- Collaboration with local governments and organisations to identify and prioritise areas in need.

3. Incorporation of SCS's Surveillance System:

- Integration of SCS's advanced surveillance system into the CT infrastructure.
- Installation of 4k cameras throughout the CT as part of a comprehensive security and monitoring solution.
- Use of CT as a role model and demonstration site to showcase the benefits of SCS's surveillance system to other governments.

4. Role Model and Demo-Display:

- Positioning the initial CT as a showcase for the effectiveness of both the modular building system and the integrated surveillance system.
- Hosting tours and presentations for government officials and stakeholders from other regions and countries.

- Marketing CT as a turnkey solution for rapid, secure, and scalable urban development.

Goals:

- Provide affordable and efficient housing solutions in rural areas.
- Demonstrate the practicality and effectiveness of modular construction.
- Showcase the integration of advanced surveillance systems for enhanced security.
- Promote the adoption of CT and SCS's solutions by other governments worldwide.

Next Steps:

1. Finalise the design and production process for the modular building pieces.
2. Set up production facilities and establish supply chain logistics.
3. Collaborate with SCS to integrate the surveillance system into the CT infrastructure.
4. Launch the initial CT as a demo-display and begin marketing to other governments.

By leveraging innovative construction techniques and advanced surveillance technology, the ChinaTown initiative aims to revolutionize housing solutions in rural areas, providing a scalable model that can be replicated globally.

Social Credit Score/SCS

1. **Integration of Social Credit Score (SCS) System:**
   - ○ **Surveillance Infrastructure:**
     - ■ Implementation of 4K cameras throughout CT for comprehensive monitoring.
   - ○ **MMORPG Elements:**
     - ■ Introduction of a Social Credit Score system where citizens earn points for various tasks and behaviours.
     - ■ Creation of a rewards system where accumulated points translate into real-life benefits (e.g., discounts, privileges).
   - ○ **Government Collaboration:**
     - ■ Partnering with local and national governments to incorporate the SCS system into their operations.

- Ensuring data privacy and security measures are in place to protect citizens.

2. **Role Model and Demo-Display:**
   - **Showcase Site:**
     - Positioning the initial CT as a showcase for both the modular building system and the integrated SCS system.
     - Hosting tours and presentations for government officials and stakeholders from other regions and countries.
   - **Marketing and Promotion:**
     - Demonstrating the benefits of the CT model to encourage adoption by other governments.
     - Highlighting the scalability and adaptability of the CT and SCS systems.

Goals:

- **Housing Solutions:**
  - Provide affordable and efficient housing in rural areas through modular construction.

- **Innovative Governance:**
  - Turn real-life into an engaging MMORPG with the SCS system, incentivizing positive behaviour and community involvement.

- **Global Adoption:**
  - Showcase CT as a replicable model for rapid urban development and advanced governance systems.

Next Steps:

1. **Finalise Design and Production:**
   - Complete the design and production process for the modular building components.

2. **Set Up Infrastructure:**
   - Establish production facilities and logistics for modular components.
   - Implement the 4K camera surveillance system.

3. **Collaborate with Governments:**
   - Work with local and national governments to integrate the SCS system.
   - Ensure proper training and education on the use of the SCS system.

4. **Launch and Promote:**

   o Launch the initial CT and use it as a demo-display.

   o Market the CT model to other governments and promote its adoption.

By combining innovative construction techniques with an advanced social credit system, the ChinaTown initiative aims to revolutionise housing and governance, providing a scalable model that can be implemented worldwide.

LMC

The Vision for Medicinal Cocaine Clinics

Liberating a South American country at a time by lobbying for political movements to legalise the production and exportation of medicinal cocaine was an ambitious and visionary plan. The idea was to assemble politicians in a European country, specifically Sweden, to pioneer medicinal clinics that could evaluate the suitability of cocaine as a treatment for depression. This groundbreaking initiative would allow users from all over Europe to seek treatment in Sweden and return home with a 30-day supply of the medicine.

This initiative aimed not only to revolutionise the treatment of depression but also to generate substantial tourist revenue for Sweden. By positioning itself as a leader in innovative mental health treatments, Sweden could attract patients and their families, boosting the local economy and enhancing its global reputation in healthcare.

The logistics involved shipping cocaine from South America to China, where it would be placed in GPS-chipped, usable containers. These containers would then be securely transported to Sweden, ensuring that the supply chain was transparent and accountable at every step.

The medicinal cocaine clinics, along with pharmacies and psychiatrists, would be housed in a specially designated area in northern Sweden, known as ChinaTown (CT). This area would be equipped with state-of-the-art facilities and comprehensive security measures to ensure the safe and ethical administration of treatment. By integrating advanced surveillance systems with 4K cameras, the CT would serve as a role model and demonstration site for other governments considering similar initiatives.

RSP

Before I heard the news about the invasion of Ukraine, I had a plan called the Russian Swedish Police (RSP). The reasoning behind this plan stemmed from the vulnerabilities in the open recruitment of police officers in Sweden. My concern was that this system could easily lead to corruption, as there have been countless instances where police officers, associated with criminal enterprises, failed to uphold their duties and did favours for criminals.

The plan involved establishing a training centre (CT) on the western side of Russia, across the ocean from Sweden. In this CT, Russian military personnel would be trained to become Swedish police officers. The training would include education in Swedish policing practices and the Swedish language. This way, by the time they arrived in Sweden, they would be fully equipped to perform their duties effectively. Additionally, this initiative aimed to improve relations between Sweden and Russia.

3K

The 3K operation was a bold and unprecedented initiative aimed at curbing the dangers of criminality in

Swedish society and reducing the profits of criminal enterprises. The plan involved a collaboration between the Swedish military and the Russian Swedish Police (RSP) to lead a large-scale operation focused on the sale of narcotics.

The operation would begin with the importation of 50 tonnes of various strains of cannabis from the Sinaloa Cartel. This would be transported via a Boeing 747 airplane, with full media coverage to highlight the groundbreaking and historical changes about to take place in Sweden. The goal was to establish a transparent, state-controlled narcotics trade that could undermine illegal markets and redirect profits to more constructive societal use.

To facilitate this, apartments designated for sales operations would be set up in every major city across Sweden. These locations would function similarly to criminal enterprises but with a crucial difference: the Swedish military would provide the muscle and oversight, ensuring that the operations were conducted safely and efficiently.

This approach was designed to minimise the dangers associated with illegal drug trade, such as violence and exploitation, while also undercutting the financial incentives that drive such activities. By taking control of the narcotics market, the Swedish government could better regulate and monitor the distribution and use of cannabis, potentially leading to a significant reduction in criminal activity and its associated harms.

However, the plan faced numerous ethical and legal challenges. The government would need to justify this approach to the public and the international community, addressing concerns about the potential normalisation of drug use and the risks associated with state involvement in the narcotics trade. Despite these challenges, the 3K operation represented a bold attempt to rethink traditional approaches to drug enforcement and public safety, something that will become possible in this era seeing as my generation is growing up to be the ones in charge of society.

EWATCH: A Revolutionary Smartwatch Concept

Introduction Inspired by my initials, EWACH—Ernst-William Axel Clifford Hertz—I envision creating a groundbreaking electronic watch named either EWACH or EWATCH. This smartwatch aims to revolutionise personal health and productivity by integrating advanced features tailored to the modern lifestyle.

Features and Functions

1. **Health Monitoring:**
   - ○ **Sleep Tracking**: EWACH monitors your sleep patterns, providing insights into the quality and duration of your rest. It helps you understand your sleep cycles and offers tips for improving sleep hygiene.
   - ○ **Heart Rate Monitoring**: The watch continuously tracks your heart rate, alerting you to any irregularities and helping you maintain optimal cardiovascular health.
   - ○ **Step Counter**: EWACH counts your daily steps, encouraging you to stay active and reach your fitness goals. It also tracks other physical activities, such as running and cycling.

2. **AI-Integrated Language Practice:**
   - ○ **Language Learning App**: The watch comes with an integrated AI app designed to help you practise and learn new languages. Using advanced speech recognition and interactive exercises, the app adapts to your proficiency level and offers personalised lessons.

○ **Real-Time Translation**: EWACH features a real-time translation tool, making it easier to communicate while travelling or interacting with speakers of different languages.

3. **Additional Smartwatch Features:**

   ○ **Notifications and Alerts**: Receive notifications for calls, messages, and social media directly on your wrist. Customise alerts to prioritise important contacts and apps.

   ○ **Fitness Goals and Reminders**: Set fitness goals and receive reminders to stay active, hydrate, and take breaks throughout the day.

   ○ **Customizable Watch Faces**: Choose from a variety of watch faces to match your style and preferences. The watch also supports third-party watch face designs.

Design and Usability

EWACH combines sleek design with user-friendly functionality. The watch features a high-resolution touch screen, durable materials, and an adjustable band for a comfortable fit. The intuitive interface allows users to easily navigate through features and settings.

Conclusion

EWACH is more than just a smartwatch; it's a personal assistant dedicated to enhancing your health, productivity, and overall well-being. By integrating health monitoring, language learning, and essential smartwatch functions, EWACH aims to become an indispensable part of your daily routine. Stay tuned for the launch of EWACH, where innovation meets elegance in wearable technology.

No Game No Life (NGNL): A Life-Enhancing Application

Introduction No Game No Life (NGNL) is an innovative application designed to gamify personal development and everyday activities. Drawing inspiration from the MMORPG Runescape's skill-menu system, NGNL tracks and showcases your "experience" in various subjects and skills, encouraging continuous growth and engagement in all aspects of life. To participate actively in NGNL, users need an EWATCH, which seamlessly integrates with the application.

Core Features

1. **Skill Menu System:**

    o **Physical Education:** Track and improve your physical fitness through various activities such as running, swimming, yoga, and more. Earn experience points (XP) for every activity, level up your physical fitness skill, and receive badges and rewards.

    o **Language Learning:** Enhance your linguistic abilities by practising new languages. The skill menu includes lessons, quizzes, and real-time conversation practice. Progress is tracked, and users earn XP as they improve their language proficiency.

    o **Social Credit Score:** Monitor and improve your social interactions and community involvement. Earn points for activities like volunteering, participating in community events, and helping others. This feature promotes positive social behaviour and community engagement.

    o **Habits & Patterns:** Develop and maintain healthy habits by tracking daily routines. Whether it's drinking water, meditating, or reading, users earn XP for consistently following good habits. The app provides reminders and insights to help build and maintain these patterns.

2. **Integration with EWATCH:**

   o **Seamless Synchronisation**: The EWATCH tracks your activities, heart rate, sleep patterns, and more, syncing this data automatically with NGNL. This integration ensures accurate tracking of your progress in various skills.

   o **Real-Time Feedback**: Receive real-time feedback and notifications on your EWATCH. Whether you've completed a daily goal or need a reminder to stay active, EWATCH keeps you informed and motivated.

3. **Gamified Experience:**

   o **Achievements and Rewards**: Unlock achievements and earn rewards as you level up in different skills. Compete with friends and other users on leaderboards, adding a competitive edge to personal development.

   o **Quests and Challenges**: Participate in quests and challenges designed to push your limits and help you gain new experiences.

Complete daily, weekly, and monthly challenges to earn additional XP and exclusive rewards.

○ **Customizable Avatars**: Personalise your in-app avatar, which evolves as you gain more experience. This feature adds a fun, visual representation of your progress.

4. **Community and Social Features:**

○ **Friend Lists and Social Feeds**: Connect with friends, share your achievements, and support each other's progress. The social feed allows users to post updates, achievements, and motivational messages.

○ **Team Challenges and Group Activities**: Form teams with friends or join public groups to tackle larger challenges. Collaborative tasks and group achievements foster a sense of community and shared goals.

Conclusion

No Game No Life transforms personal development into an engaging and rewarding experience. By leveraging the capabilities of the EWATCH and the gamified structure of NGNL, users are motivated to continuously improve their skills and habits. Whether you're aiming to get fit, learn a new language, or become more socially active, NGNL makes the journey enjoyable and fulfilling. Join the NGNL community and start levelling up your life today!

BestBuds (BB): A Vision Reborn

Introduction BestBuds (BB) was my treasure, a venture with a vision to revolutionise the European cannabis market. At its peak, I owned 17 domain names, including a fully translated website for the Chinese market, thanks to my partner in Xi'An, Phil Huang. We had a diverse range of products manufactured globally: CBD snus and rolling papers from China, blunt cones from India, and CBD and melatonin e-juice from Sweden. Though the enterprise has scaled down, I retain the Swedish and Finnish domain names, BestBuds.se and BestBuds.fi, and the Instagram handle BestBudsAB, along with the crucial contacts to reignite this endeavour.

Product Line

1. **CBD Snus and Rolling Papers:**
   - ○ **Manufactured in China:** High-quality CBD snus offering a smokeless alternative for CBD consumption. The rolling papers,

designed for ease and durability, cater to both novice and seasoned users.

2. **Blunt Cones**:
   - **Manufactured in India**: Premium blunt cones crafted to enhance the smoking experience. These are made from natural, sustainable materials, ensuring a smooth and enjoyable session every time.

3. **CBD and Melatonin E-Juice**:
   - **Manufactured in Sweden**: Innovative e-juice blends that combine the calming effects of CBD with the sleep-inducing properties of melatonin. Ideal for users looking to unwind and improve their sleep quality.

Current Assets

- **Domain Names**: BestBuds.se and BestBuds.fi, serving the Swedish and Finnish markets.
- **Social Media Presence**: Instagram account BestBudsAB, a platform to connect with customers, share updates, and promote products.

- **Contact Network**: A well-established network of manufacturers and partners ready to collaborate and bring the enterprise back to life.

Strategic Plan for Relaunch

1. **Market Analysis and Strategy**:
   - **Identify Target Markets**: Focus on regions with growing acceptance and demand for CBD products, particularly in Europe.
   - **Competitor Analysis**: Study existing players in the market to identify gaps and opportunities.

2. **Product Development and Quality Control**:
   - **Enhance Product Line**: Expand the product range to include new CBD-infused items, ensuring compliance with local regulations.
   - **Quality Assurance**: Implement stringent quality control measures to maintain high standards across all products.

3. **Branding and Marketing**:
   - **Rebrand and Relaunch**: Develop a compelling brand story that resonates with the European Cannabis Movement. Utilise social media and other digital marketing

channels to create buzz and attract customers.

- ○ **Collaborations and Partnerships**: Partner with influencers, health professionals, and cannabis advocates to promote the brand and educate the public on the benefits of CBD.

4. **Logistics and Distribution**:

- ○ **Efficient Supply Chain**: Leverage the existing contact network to streamline manufacturing and distribution processes.
- ○ **Local Partnerships**: Establish partnerships with local distributors and retailers to ensure widespread availability of products.

5. **Customer Engagement and Feedback**:

- ○ **Build a Community**: Foster a sense of community among customers through engaging content, events, and loyalty programs.
- ○ **Continuous Improvement**: Gather customer feedback to continually refine products and services.

Conclusion

BestBuds is poised to make a triumphant return as a leading advocate and provider in the European cannabis market. With a solid foundation, strategic vision, and the right partnerships, BB can once again become a beacon for quality and innovation in the CBD industry. The journey begins anew, with the potential to create a significant impact and drive the European Cannabis Movement forward.

JuraMajs Crepes Wagons

One of my business ventures involves importing and managing my former employer's Danish business, JuraMajs Crepes Wagons, into Sweden and Bornholm. The concept is to bring the beloved crepes and their unique flavours to a new audience, expanding the business across borders and tapping into the potential of new markets. Here's what we need to make this happen:

1. **A Storage Unit**
   - A secure storage unit is essential for housing supplies, ingredients, and equipment. It needs to be centrally located to ensure easy access for distribution and restocking of the crepe wagons. The unit

must meet food safety standards to keep all materials in optimal condition.

2. **Personnel**

   ○ Hiring a dedicated team is crucial for the successful operation of JuraMajs Crepes Wagons. We need experienced and enthusiastic personnel who are passionate about food and customer service. This includes:

   - **Crepe Makers**: Skilled in preparing and cooking crepes to perfection.

   - **Logistics Coordinators**: Responsible for overseeing the distribution of supplies and maintenance of the wagons.

   - **Managers**: To supervise operations, ensure quality control, and handle administrative tasks.

3. **A Location with a Permit**

   ○ Securing a prime location with the necessary permits is critical. This involves:

   - **Scouting Locations**: Finding high-traffic areas where the crepe wagons can attract the most customers. This includes popular streets, parks, markets, and events.

- **Obtaining Permits**: Navigating the local regulations to acquire the appropriate permits for operating food wagons. This includes health and safety permits, business licenses, and any other required documentation.
- **Establishing a Base**: Setting up a central location where the wagons can be prepped, restocked, and maintained.

Bringing JuraMajs Crepes Wagons to Sweden and Bornholm is not just about expanding a business; it's about sharing a culinary experience that has delighted many in Denmark. With careful planning and execution, this venture can become a beloved addition to the local food scene in these new markets.

The plans I had meticulously crafted, the dreams I'd woven into every pitch and every sleepless night, felt like lifelines to a brighter future. BestBuds wasn't just a business to me—it was redemption. It was a way to prove to the world, and perhaps even to myself, that I could create something meaningful out of chaos.

But life has a way of twisting narratives, pulling you from ambition to reckoning with little warning. Just as the seeds of my enterprise began to sprout, reality closed in, pulling me back to the unresolved. The weight of Santiago Martínez's murder, the evidence, and the growing shadows of suspicion loomed larger than I had anticipated.

I was no longer just a man chasing a dream; I was a man facing a courtroom, the scales of justice poised to decide my fate. The business plans, the partnerships, the promises—all of it would have to wait. My story was now on trial.

Court

It was time for court. The morning began with the harsh clinking of keys as the transportation officers unlocked my cell door. They gave me the usual curt instructions, and soon I found myself being escorted to the waiting transportation vehicle. The ride was silent except for the hum of the engine and the occasional murmur of the guards, a constant reminder of the gravity of the day ahead.

Upon arrival at the courthouse, I was led to a temporary holding cell. The cold, stark walls offered no comfort, just a brief pause before the storm. A court-appointed officer entered, carrying a neatly folded set of clothes my mother had lovingly chosen for me. The suit was modest but professional—her way of saying, *stand tall, no matter what happens.*

I ran my fingers over the fabric, feeling a pang of guilt and gratitude. I changed quickly, the transformation oddly grounding me in the surreal nature of the day. The stark prison clothes were gone, replaced by something that reminded me of a life I was desperate to hold onto, even as it seemed to slip further from my grasp.

The moments in the cell stretched endlessly, every sound amplifying my nerves—the faint echo of footsteps, the distant murmur of voices. Then came the knock, and the door creaked open. It was time to face the courtroom, the judge and the verdict that could shape the rest of my life.

The courtroom was silent except for the soft shuffle of papers and the rhythmic ticking of the clock. I sat in the defendant's chair, my expression composed yet unreadable. The prosecutor, sharp-eyed and methodical, rose to address the court. Her tone was deliberate, each word carefully chosen to paint a picture of premeditated violence.

"Your Honour," she began, holding up a series of photographs for the jury to see, "these are the bloody clothes found in the washing machine at Santiago Martínez's residence. They were still stained because the machine, stuck between programs, never started. This, along with other forensic evidence, ties the defendant to the crime scene."

I watched her intently, calculating my every reaction. Inside, my thoughts were racing. Should I come clean and expose everything—the connections, the circumstances, the unspoken truths? Should I bring Ann-Marie forward as a witness to corroborate parts of my story and salvage what little dignity I had left? No. That would only complicate things.

I realized it was better to maintain my silence. Let the narrative spiral as it may. If I played my cards right, the psychiatric ward was a far better alternative than prison.

I couldn't help but feel utterly stupid and ridiculous as the witness statements piled up, painting me as some kind of monster. The courtroom echoed with fabricated accounts of how I had drugged and sexually harassed friends of Santiago, each story more absurd than the last. It felt like I was being tried for crimes I couldn't even fathom committing, crimes that didn't just challenge my character but sought to annihilate it entirely.

They had elevated Santiago to sainthood, a narrative that painted him as a kind soul who had graciously housed a homeless man—a mentally disabled individual. The so-called *Saintiago* everyone spoke of wasn't the man I knew. This wasn't the scheming, conniving parasite who used his supposed handicap as a ruse to cheat the system.

No, the Santiago I knew had crafted an image of himself so meticulously that even now, after his death, it was serving him well. And somehow, I was the one left paying the price for his performance.

The weight of their words pressed down on me, but what angered me most wasn't the lies themselves—it was the people willing to believe them. They didn't know the real Santiago, the one who had exploited the goodwill of others and manipulated the system with ease. And now, as the prosecution piled on their evidence and dramatic storytelling, I was left in the impossible position of defending myself against their saintly fabrication.

The irony wasn't lost on me: I had killed a man who built his life on lies, and yet, in the public's eyes, it was my truth that was now under trial.

He had carefully painted up a picture of himself as a handicapped individual to cheat the system and now I had to pay for it.

The prosecutor continued, bringing up a witness—the Columbian sister of Santiago. She recounted her version of events, her gaze flickering toward me. At one point, she raised her hand and slowly drew her finger across her throat, a silent, chilling gesture meant to intimidate. The courtroom gasped softly, but I didn't flinch. Instead, I locked eyes with her, maintaining an unsettling calm, as if her theatrics were beneath my notice.

When it was my lawyer's turn, she rose with a quiet confidence that filled the room. "Your Honor, the defense would like to remind the court that all of this evidence is circumstantial. My client has consistently maintained that he spent the night on Santiago's couch and has no knowledge of the events that transpired thereafter."

She wove a narrative of doubt, pointing out the lack of concrete evidence directly tying me to the act itself. Her arguments were compelling, and I appreciated how fervently she seemed to believe in my innocence—or perhaps just in her own abilities as a defence lawyer.

Despite her best efforts, I could see the jury's curiosity shift as they studied me. My erratic behaviour during earlier interrogations—muttering nonsense and appearing disconnected—had laid the groundwork for the defence's strategy of mental instability. But the calm demeanour I now displayed was a double-edged sword. Was it the composure of a calculated mind or the calm of someone mentally detached from reality? The court seemed divided.

The thought of speaking up lingered for a moment longer. I pictured myself addressing the court, telling the full truth, and dragging others into the fray. Ann-Marie, Gloria, Nava—names that would ripple through the courtroom and beyond. But I knew better. My silence was my shield. Prison was a dead end; the psychiatric ward held a glimmer of hope, however faint.

So I sat there, letting the weight of the prosecutor's accusations and the sharpness of my lawyer's counterarguments swirl around me. The performance had begun long before the trial, and I wasn't about to break character now.

Author's Note

I write this book not to glorify my choices but to illuminate the shadows of my past, to prevent others from stumbling into the same pitfalls that have defined much of my life. If there's one thing I've learned, it's that the paths we choose are often shaped by desperation, pain, and circumstances that feel beyond our control.

I wish things could have been different. I wish there had been another way to resolve what had happened— one that didn't involve violence, pain, or the irreversible weight of taking a life. But in my case, with all that I knew and all that I felt, I couldn't see another way. At that moment, murder wasn't just an option; it felt like the only way forward.

Looking back, I often wonder: Was there a choice I didn't see? Was there a road I could have taken that would have spared everyone, including myself, from the aftermath? I'll never know. But through this book, I hope to give others the tools, the warnings, and the wisdom to see those roads before it's too late.

Desperate to find a way out, I turned my focus back to legitimate business ventures. The transition was anything but smooth. Trust was hard to come by, and my criminal record was a constant barrier. Yet, I persisted, channelling all my energy into creating detailed business plans and seeking out opportunities that aligned with my vision for a better future.

That's when I began with the idea of BestBuds. A legal corporation that could double up as a smuggling joint.

The road to redemption was long and arduous. It required confronting my past, making amends where possible, and finding a way to reconcile the different parts of my identity. The plans I drafted during my time in custody were a testament to this journey—a blend of ambition, regret, and an unyielding desire to make something of my life.

As I look back, I see a story of survival and transformation. My entry into the world of crime was a detour, a dark chapter that tested my limits and ultimately shaped my resolve to find a better path. It is a part of my story, but not the end. Each step forward is a reminder of where I've been and where I aspire to go.

I sit here in the quiet confines of the psychiatric ward in Falköping, Sweden, and I am surrounded by the echoes of my past, every word in this book a testament to the road I've travelled. These memoirs are not fiction. Every event, every choice, and every consequence are rooted in the reality I've lived.

Writing this has been both a catharsis and a confrontation—a way to lay bare the truth not only for myself but for others who might find themselves on a similar path. My story is not a glorification of crime or chaos; it is a cautionary tale, one I hope will resonate deeply with parents, children, and communities alike.

My hope is to prevent other families from experiencing the devastation of organized crime. The allure of fast money and a sense of belonging can be overwhelming, but it comes at a cost that few are prepared to pay. Families are torn apart, futures are derailed, and lives are lost.

Above all, I wish to emphasize the importance of honesty. Parents must create spaces where their children feel safe to speak up—where admitting to struggles, whether with narcotics or other issues, is met with compassion rather than condemnation. These conversations could make the difference between intervention and tragedy, between a second chance and a life defined by regret.

To anyone reading this, know that change is always possible. While the weight of my choices remains, I choose to hope that sharing my story might save someone else from making the same mistakes. And if even one person reconsiders their path, then this journey—my journey—will not have been in vain.

I'm contemplating whether I should change my name entirely, get a protected identity when I leave this place— so I can start fresh. A life free from crime and drugs, where I can pursue a meaningful education, secure a stable job, and eventually build a family of my own.

It feels overwhelming at times, thinking about all the bridges I've burned and the mess I've left behind. But maybe a clean slate is what I need, a chance to prove to myself and others that I'm capable of more. Starting over doesn't erase the past, but it gives me the opportunity to reshape my future into something worth living for.

I want to build something steady and real. A life where I don't have to look over my shoulder or feel the weight of my mistakes every single day. A place to belong, people to share it with, and the satisfaction of knowing I've left behind the chaos for something good, something honest.

Rest in Peace, K-O and Amin Kazaz

To K-O and Amin Kazaz, two souls whose journeys ended far too soon, may you both rest in eternal peace.

K-O, your laughter, energy, and unwavering loyalty left an imprint on everyone fortunate enough to cross paths with you. You stood tall in the face of challenges, bringing light into the darkest of moments.

Amin, your kindness and charisma were unmatched. A pillar of strength to those who knew you, you had the unique ability to connect with people from all walks of life. Your presence was magnetic, and your absence is deeply felt.

The memories we shared serve as a reminder of the fleeting nature of life and the impact one can leave behind. Though you both may be gone, you are far from forgotten. You live on in the stories we tell, the lessons we've learned, and the bonds we continue to cherish.

Rest easy, brothers. Your legacies will remain etched in our hearts forever.

Rest in Peace, Leks

To my dear friend Leks,

Thank you for the kindness you showed me when I needed it most. In Leuven, you took me into your home, offering not only a roof over my head but also a sense of belonging. You guided me in ways I'll never forget, and your presence during those challenging times was a light in the darkness.

You took me under your wing when the world felt chaotic, and your generosity, laughter, and unwavering support left an indelible mark on my life. I will forever be grateful for the moments we shared, from late-night talks to simply navigating life together.

It breaks my heart to know that your light has dimmed, that the world lost you to a battle you shouldn't have faced alone. Your passing reminds me, and should remind all of us, just how important it is to prioritize mental health and reach out to those who may be struggling. Suicide prevention isn't just a concept—it's a lifeline we must extend to one another.

To anyone reading this: if you or someone you know is struggling, don't stay silent. Reach out, listen, and show up. Sometimes a simple conversation can make all the difference.

Rest in peace, Leks. You will forever be missed, and your memory will live on in my heart.

With gratitude and sorrow,

Hugo

Acknowledgements

This is a list of people who made it possible for me to continue striving to live and thus enabling this book being written.

Sinaloa cartel for giving me a purpose in life.

Karl-Johan Wallander for reading through this book and giving me pointers, helping me to actually get this done.

My mother, **Pia Andersson** for always being there for me and raising me to the extent where I get praised for being well-mannered.

My father, **Peter Hertz** for all of his help in my life. I wish you the best of luck with your company, ClimateCurtainsAB.

Mission for helping me sober up from a heroin addiction, taking me in when I was sleeping on the streets and genuinely being there for me when I needed it the most.

Morten Humme for providing me with a friendly environment when I was down to my knees and needed some positive energy.

I want to thank both **Fares Tillo** and **Jozsef Lakatos** for helping me out through a stressful time at the psychiatric ward.

To **the Hungarian Mafia & Nathe** for giving me refugee when I had been "kidnapped".

Shooter Gang for their music. Also, shoutout to Hov1!

Pia Lerigon for helping me with the process of writing a book through her e-course.

Additionally, **Audrey, Elle, and Thomas,**

I wanted to take a moment to express my deepest gratitude for everything you've done to *bring Memoirs from the Psych Ward* to life. From the thoughtful edits to the meticulous formatting and invaluable guidance throughout the publishing process, your support has been nothing short of extraordinary.

Audrey, your insightful feedback and passion for the project have elevated the book in ways I couldn't have imagined. Your ability to see its potential and refine its essence has been a gift. Elle, your precision and attention to detail during formatting have ensured the book looks and reads beautifully. And Thomas, your professionalism and clear communication have made navigating this entire journey smooth and stress-free.

Together, you've not only helped me tell my story but have also given me the confidence to share it with the world. Your dedication and expertise have made this dream a reality, and I cannot thank you enough for being part of this transformative journey.

I'm truly grateful for your hard work and belief in this project. I look forward to seeing Hatake Hugo out in the world and continuing to collaborate with you all in the future.

Warmest regards,

Ernst-William Hertz